The Lighter Side

An NHS Paramedic's Selection of Humorous Mess Room Tales

Andy Thompson

Published in February 2016 by emp3books,
Norwood House, Elvetham Road, Fleet, GU51 4HL, England

ISBN: 978-1-910734-11-7

*****

Also Available in Paperback, Digital and Audio Format

The Dark Side

Real Life Accounts of an NHS Paramedic

The Good, the Bad and the Downright Ugly

The Dark Side

Part 2

Real Life Accounts of an NHS Paramedic

The Traumatic, the Tragic and the Tearful

www.andythompson-author.com

Contents

Dedication

This book is dedicated to the lady, whom shall remain nameless, for officially complaining to the NHS Ambulance Service, after she spotted two ambulance personnel laughing in the cab of their ambulance while responding to an emergency using blue lights and sirens. Her grievance was that she failed to see how anything could be funny working in the Accident and Emergency Services, and was therefore disgusted by what she witnessed.

A message for the complainant on behalf of all ambulance personnel around the globe: You couldn't be more wrong!

Acknowledgements

I would like to thank professional copy-editor, *Kevin O'Byrne* (www.aspiringauthors.co.uk). His exceptional editing and proofreading skills, which in my opinion are second to none, and his input and being a sounding board for advice, has enabled me to give the reader an insightful, legible and pleasurable reading experience once again. I would also like to thank *Richard Duszczak* (www.cartoonstudio.co.uk), for the professional cartoon drawing used to design this book's front cover, and also for the cartoon drawings that accompany each anecdote throughout this book.

Prologue

The following selection of humorous tales portrays the *'Lighter Side'* of working on *'The Dark Side'* of the NHS Ambulance Service. I must confess, though, that I was party to only *some* of the incidents that follow, and so can only confirm that those particular incidents genuinely occurred. The remainder I heard second or third hand during downtime with my fellow colleagues in the mess room of various ambulance stations, so I've written the stories as accurately as I can remember them being recited to me, including the dialogue, though I do not profess it to be verbatim.

About the Author

In June 2002, Andy commenced employment with the Mersey Regional Ambulance Service, which later merged with the Cumbria, Greater Manchester and Lancashire Ambulance Services to form the Northwest Ambulance Service NHS Trust. He rapidly progressed from the Patient Transport Service (PTS) to qualified Paramedic status via Ambulance Technician training, experience gained in the job and further extended training from which, upon qualifying, he was presented with a 'Professional Paramedic Development Award' for most improved candidate.

In 2005 he registered with the Health Professions Council (HPC), the national governing body for UK paramedics; this changed its name to the Health and Care Professions Council (HCPC) in August 2012.

Andy spent the earlier part of his career working in the English counties of Cheshire and Merseyside. In 2007, after living 'up north' for 32 years, Andy relocated down south with his wife and two children, residing there until he and his family relocated to North Yorkshire in September 2013. There, Andy continued his career as an NHS Paramedic with the Yorkshire Ambulance Service until October 2015.

Content that he'd enjoyed an incredibly rewarding career, and very proud to have saved many lives and made a significant difference to countless others, Andy decided to 'hang up' his stethoscope and explore other projects. He currently spends the majority of his working week doing what he enjoys the most... writing.

To read more about the author, please visit: www.andythompson-author.com

Foreword

I'm honoured to be able to write this foreword for my good friend and former colleague, Andy Thompson. It's been a couple of years now since we last had the opportunity to work together 'on the road'. I miss the patient interactions that I used to have while working alongside Andy, which were altogether memorable and often very comical as, apart from sharing the same surname, we also share a very similar sense of humour. Together, we were often referred to as a modern day *Smith and Jones*, as we'd inject humour at any given opportunity and frequently 'bounce' spontaneous witticisms off each other, both on and off duty.

In the paramedical profession, we strive to deliver the very best care we can provide for our patients, and they rely upon us to be one hundred percent focused on our duties. That said, there are many occasions where humour provides a viable alternative to Entonox or IV Morphine for the reduction of pain, and in the delivery of patient reassurance. It's curious, but when you arrive at patients' 'bedsides', figuratively speaking, you very quickly gauge the measure of the patient and make a distinction between those who will not respond well to humour, and those that will appreciate and respond positively to it.

I have read all of Andy's books, and I, along with many other ambulance personnel, can relate to the humorous anecdotes contained within this book. Andy and I experienced many, many humorous incidences working alongside each other as an ambulance crew; one in particular, which had us both in stitches and crying with laughter, is included in this book. This book really does emphasise the 'Lighter Side' of the profession and accentuates that the job isn't always sombre, and also why possessing a sense of humour is a necessary aspect of the role, to enable us to cope with everyday life, whether we're on operational duty in a professional capacity, or not.

Graham Thompson BSc (Hons) – Emergency Care Practitioner (ECP)

Introduction

Laughter is contagious. The sheer sound of someone laughing out loud is far more infectious than any airborne virus or bacterial infection. When laughter is shared, it brings people together and increases joy and happiness. Laughter also produces healthy physical changes in the body, and shields you from the damaging effects of stress and anxiety. That's right, laughter is a powerful medicine for stress. There's nothing that works faster to bring your mind and body back into balance than a flamin' good belly laugh. A good belly laugh also boosts the immune system and increases immune cells and antibodies, thus improving your resistance to infection.

Laughter also triggers the release of endorphins, the body's own natural 'Happy Pill', and protects the heart by improving the function of blood vessels and increasing blood flow, which can help protect you against a heart attack and other cardiovascular problems. With so much influence to heal and renew, the ability to laugh effortlessly, and often, is a fantastic resource for overcoming difficulties, improving your relationships, and supporting physical, mental and emotional health.

More than just respite from unhappiness, discomfort and pain, laughter gives you the power and courage to find a fresh source of optimism. Even in the most demanding of times, a laugh, or even just a smile, can have a huge impact on your overall wellbeing. Greatest of all, this invaluable medicine is not only fun, it's also free!

With all that said, I decided to write this book to accompany and conclude my *'The Dark Side – Real Life Accounts of an NHS Paramedic'* series, and share with you, the reader, *some* of the many humorous accounts that have emerged and circulated from ambulance personnel's experiences. Reciting those experiences in the mess room of ambulance stations, with colleagues, is significant in creating the unique camaraderie that exists amongst ambulance personnel around the globe.

I would like to add the caveat that if you find any of the following stories insensitive, crude or distasteful, then please accept my sincere apologies. However, before you criticise, judge or condemn ambulance personnel as being insensitive or unprofessional, please bear in mind that the vast majority of health care professionals are very caring and compassionate people. At the same time, from the start of their career many, though not all, ambulance personnel tend to gradually develop a dark sense of humour... if they don't already possess it. Possessing a dark sense of humour is not considered insensitive or unprofessional in ambulance service culture; it is simply a coping mechanism and is *usually* only revealed away from the eyes and ears of the patient or members of the public in general.

Now, I appreciate people's sense of humour differs, and I'm glad that it does, because as the late English Philosopher, Sir *Bernard Arthur Owen Williams,* quoted: *"What a strange world this would be if we all had the same sense of humour."* Nevertheless, I do hope the following stories provide you with some laugh out loud moments, prompt you to take a gasp with shock, or raise a smile at the very least.

Note from the author: This book was written, produced and edited in the UK where spellings and word usage can vary from the U.S. English. The use of quotes in dialogue and other punctuation can also differ.

Andy Thompson

The Lighter Side

An NHS Paramedic's Selection of Humorous Mess Room Tales

A Poor Choice of Words

There are incidences when you say something completely inappropriate, using a poor choice of words at an incredibly inappropriate time, aren't there? We've all done it, I'm sure. I know I have, on numerous occasions. This incident involved a frail, elderly lady and two experienced female members of the Patient Transport Service (PTS), Gill and Ellie.

They had arrived at the old lady's house to convey her to her outpatient appointment. However, before they could assist the barely mobile patient arm in arm to the ambulance, the lady politely announced that she needed to use the bathroom before they left, as she wouldn't be able to hold on, so to speak, until she got to hospital. So, Gill assisted the lady toward the bathroom. On entering the bathroom, the old lady ruffled her dress up, pulled her underwear down and proceeded to empty her bladder... sorry, was that too much information?!

Anyway, moments later, her crewmate Ellie, stood outside of the bathroom, heard Gill say,

'Oh, what a lovely pussy! Did you have that professionally groomed?'

Horrified, Ellie cringed at the extremely unprofessional comment to make to anybody, let alone a frail old lady. It was only after they'd conveyed the patient to the hospital that Ellie was able to ask Gill about her inappropriate remark. After a thoughtful moment or two while Gill realised how it must have sounded, and with a smile beginning to form on her lips, she was then able to explain just what had prompted her to admire the old lady's pussy.

Upon entering the bathroom with the old dear, she couldn't fail to notice that the lady had numerous framed photographs displayed on the bathroom walls, and while the lady was having a wee, Gill was admiring the pictures, impressed by one in particular that had a 'fit for a queen' appearance. They were pictures of her, now deceased, cats.

Having clarified to Ellie exactly what she had meant by the comment, and with the pair now both contemplating every detail of the cringe-worthy misunderstanding, they could barely stop chuckling to themselves for the rest of their entire shift.

What a Way to Go!

My colleague and I were dispatched to attend to an elderly male in cardiac arrest. His wife had found him in the lounge when she got home from a long shopping trip, and so rang treble-nine. When we arrived, we quickly ascertained, by his rigor-mortised state, that he'd been dead for some time. Oddly at first, we found him lying on his back on the floor, with a swivel office chair beneath him. It appeared as if he had tipped backwards on it. There was the whirring sound of a computer switched on. His PC monitor was idle and so the screensaver image was visible, showing countless three dimensional moving stars projecting across the screen.

I tactfully informed the patient's wife that, sadly, her husband had died, and then contacted ambulance control and requested the police to attend on behalf of the coroner's office. His wife, obviously distraught, sat herself at a dining table in the adjoining kitchen, while my colleague sat next to her and completed the relevant documentation. While he was doing that, something dawned on me; that the patient had evidently fallen backwards while doing some computer-based task, such as browsing the internet. So, discreetly, without alerting his wife to my 'snooping', I nudged the keyboard mouse so the computer came back to life from its idle mode. There, to my surprise, I found myself faced with a screen filled by the unmistakeable images of a hard-core pornography website.

Putting two-and-two together, I looked back down at the deceased patient and noticed his trouser belt and zip were unfastened.

'Blimey!' I thought, 'I hope I've still got libido when I'm his age.' So, not wanting to upset his wife, who may or may not have known of his web surfing habits, I discreetly pressed the 'Homepage' button, removing the source and what had possibly been a contributing factor to his ill-timed death.

I know what you're thinking, that it would remain in the browsing history, but I wasn't prepared to tamper with that.

Upon the police arriving, I'd no choice but to inform them of my findings. I also had to tell my colleague to document words describing what I'd found because, embarrassing as it may have been, it could have provided pertinent evidence to a pathologist on investigating the cause of death during a post-mortem examination. In the very manner-of-fact way in which these things are conducted, the evidence might have indicated an occlusion in a coronary artery caused by the heart rate and blood pressure significantly increasing at the sight of... well, you know, 'explicit online material'. It may be that some arterial plaque became dislodged and caused a fatal cardiac arrhythmia. It's most unlikely that the pathologist would have noted it by its colloquial description: 'death by porno'.

I jest, I know next to nothing about post-mortems. But I wouldn't have been surprised if it was a heart attack that killed him while in the act of erm... master... ahem... relieving himself.

Is That Fred?

A paramedic and his crewmate were driving along the road, when up ahead they could see a cyclist riding along in the same direction as them.

'Is that Fred from our station?' the crewmate asked the driver. Straining his eyes in his attempt to confirm whether the cyclist up ahead was Fred, he said,

'Yeah, it is.'

With both of them in the mood for a bit of banter, they decided to give Fred an unwelcome acknowledgement that they'd seen him while out cycling, so the crewmate rolled up his newspaper and wound down his window.

'Slow down, slow down,' he said to the driver as they approached the cyclist from behind. When they levelled up with Fred, he leant forward out of the passenger seat and hung his arm out of the window. As they drove by, he swung his arm at the cyclist, with the rolled-up newspaper in his hand, and slapped it around the back of his head. The driver then continued on, passed the cyclist, and both crew members laughed out loud.

The offending ambulance man looked into the passenger side wing mirror, where he could see the face of the disgruntled cyclist, by now waving his fist at them. He then turned to his crewmate and, with no remorse whatsoever, casually said,

'No, we were wrong, it wasn't Fred. I haven't got a clue who that was.'

Instead of Fred, some poor sod that they didn't know, quietly enjoying a leisurely ride of his bicycle, got a slap around the back of his head with a rolled up newspaper in a pure case of mistaken identity... by an ambulance man! It wouldn't happen today, what with the standards required to possess and maintain professional registration: you would no doubt be fired, struck off the professional register and probably arrested and charged with assault. How times have changed, hey!

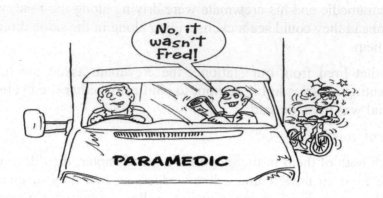

And Your Name Is?

It is said, usually using a typical northern accent, that 'there's nowt as queer as folk'. And I can vouch for that! I had to deal with an abundance of strange people throughout my career. This next incident involved a man who acted like no one I'd ever had the 'pleasure' to meet before, while on duty anyway, and who also had me and my now retired colleague in absolute stitches.

During a night shift at around midnight, my colleague, Bill, and I were dispatched to a lady in her early forties experiencing common-cold like symptoms. Upon arriving at the patient's side, Bill and I began assessing and questioning her. While doing so, a man, also in his early forties, entered the lounge where we all were. He was a short, skin-headed and stocky man that looked like a human Pit Bull terrier. I turned to face him, smiled and said,

'Evening chief, we're just assessing your wife but there doesn't seem to be any concerns so far.'

'Are you taking her to hospital?' he asked.

'I doubt it, there's really no need, from what we can gather,' I replied.

'Well I think she needs to go,' he said, sternly. Bill and I looked at each other, both acknowledging his tone.

'And your name is?' I asked.

'Sensei,' he replied.

'Bonsai?' I asked, knowing full well he'd said Sensei.

'No, not Bonsai, Sensei,' he clarified.

'Oh, right. What are you, a karate instructor or something?' I asked, with knowledge of the title.

'Yeah, Shotokan, black belt third Dan. I teach adults and kids down the community centre,' he replied with pride.

'I'm not sure you should be,' I thought, but instead said, 'Yeah but

19

you don't seriously want to be, or expect to be, addressed as Sensei outside of the dojo, do you?' He didn't answer my question; instead, to my shock, more from the ridiculous nature of his appearance than in horror, he suddenly adopted a basic Shotokan style karate stance.

'What the…?' I said with a smirk on my face, as Bill, who wasn't au fait with martial arts, stood speechless.

'Oh give over, Keith, you cock,' his wife said, as if despairing. He then came back to a normal stance… well, not 'normal', more the stance of a night club door supervisor trying to appear intimidating; you know, legs apart, shoulders back, and arms pointing straight down with hands overlapped across the groin. He then said,

'You do karate, do ya?'

'I have done, amongst other arts,' I replied.

'Yeah, you work the doors, do ya?' he asked with a curt voice and nodding his head at the same time.

'No, and I've no desire to either,' I said.

'I work the doors,' he informed me. Frowning and thinking that I wasn't sure he should be doing that either, Bill then asks him,

'Where've you worked the doors, Bonsai, T-O-T-T?'

'It's not Bonsai, it's Sensei, and yeah, I have worked at T-O-T-T,' he confirmed.

'Where else Bonsai, The Showboat?'

'It's Sensei, and yes I have.'

'Mr Smith's?'

'Yep.'

'Secrets?'

'Yep.' Then I butted in,

'Wacky Warehouse?'

'Yep,' came the immediate response.

'Coco's Play Barn?'

'Yep.'

Well, on Bonsai confirming he'd acted as 'bouncer' at the last two venues, Bill and I couldn't contain ourselves and burst out laughing. He just stood there with the bouncer-like posture, oblivious to why we were laughing. He hadn't twigged that the last two were not night clubs on the door supervisor circuit but well established children's indoor playgrounds!

Bonsai's wife didn't need a visit to the A&E and so, still grinning and occasionally giggling to myself, I completed the non-conveyance documentation. Bill and I vacated the address, leaving Bonsai's wife despairing at her husband's bizarre behaviour towards an ambulance crew. Throughout the entire journey back to the ambulance station, the pair of us could barely stop laughing. I had visions of him scuffling with a five year old boy having a tantrum in the ball pit, and trying to escort him from Coco's Play Barn before resuming that intimidating pose at the door, just below the sign of Coco, the clown.

Yep, there's nowt as queer as folk, and there's plenty of them out there, of that I'm certain!

Weaknesses

There's one thing you cannot have if you want to be a paramedic, and that is a weak stomach. You need bowels of an iron constitution so that you are able to endure the sight and smell of blood, sweat, snot; vomit, phlegm, urine; faeces, burnt flesh, open wounds, and much, much more. Every paramedic has had most of the above mentioned on their hands, sometimes even their face and/or uniform, at some point in their career. It's often unavoidable.

Paramedics tend to have the stomach for most, but a weakness for at least one of the above. My personal weakness is faeces, especially when it was under an elderly patient's finger nails or smeared across their hands, and as I'd assist them onto the carry-chair, they'd grab hold of my shirt because they thought they were going to fall. Fortunately, although my weakness, those events only caused me to retch at the very most. The rest, however, I was fine with, though I did occasionally cheat and rub a little Vicks under my nose when dealing with… an undesired smell, shall we say.

One former colleague of mine, who was a very good paramedic, had his weakness get the better of him while attending to a patient who had been deceased for several hours. Found by her son, the crew chose not to attempt resuscitation because of how long she had evidently been dead. Evidence from the bathroom, and the fact that a towel lay on her bed, suggested she had taken a bath before collapsing in the bedroom, and was therefore naked on their arrival. For that reason and out of respect, they decided that, for dignity purposes, the decent thing to do would be to lift her from the carpeted bedroom floor onto the bed and cover her modesty up with a duvet. So while the patient's son was sat downstairs, obviously upset by the loss of his mother, the crew lifted the patient using a top 'n' tail method.

As they lifted her, the deceased lady's bowels, now relaxed post-death due to the sphincter muscles becoming deprived of oxygen, emptied mid-lift from the floor toward the bed. My colleague, whose weakness was also faeces, immediately observed and smelt the contents of the patient's open bowels, and having eaten a Pot Noodle a short time before, hurled the entire contents back up, just as they were placing the patient onto the bed. As a result, he vomited all over her genitalia!

Shocked at where the regurgitated contents had landed, he pondered for a dignified solution. But, after a little thinking, he instead chose to go downstairs and tactfully explain the unfortunate calamity to the lady's son. Fortunately, he was very understanding and so told him not to worry about it.

Embarrassed by the unpleasant and unavoidable mishap, the paramedic then had to explain to the police, who attended to act on behalf of the coroner's office, why the deceased lady's genitals were covered by the contents of a chicken and sweetcorn Pot Noodle.

Misunderstandings

When ambulance personnel arrive at a patient's side and begin ascertaining the history of their present complaint, along with any past medical history, it can *sometimes* quite easily become a very confusing conversation. How the attending paramedic communicates with them can make the difference between establishing an accurate history, or not. Quite often, patients cannot accurately answer the simplest of questions. For example, the patient may be asked by the paramedic or other health care professional,

'Are you on any prescribed medication?' Simple enough question, don't you think? However, the answer paramedics often receive is similar to the following:

'No, absolutely none whatsoever. Oh, except for Metformin for my diabetes. Oh and... erm Ramipril and Simvastatin. I've got high blood pressure and high cholesterol. And then there's GTN for my angina. Oh, and I take an Aspirin every day, too.' Unbelievable!

Conversely, I may have been rummaging through a patient's prescription medication box, or browsing at their repeat prescription and asked, merely as a rhetorical question,

'I see you're on Ramipril and Simvastatin, so you have high blood pressure and high cholesterol, is that right?' The answer often received was,

'No, my blood pressure and cholesterol levels are fine according to my GP.' The usual response to that would have been,

'Then why have you been prescribed this medication by your GP?'

'Well, it's because I take that medication that my blood pressure and cholesterol are fine.'

Dipstick! That's what ambulance personnel tend to think on hearing that piece of flawed logic, but instead reply with, 'Ah, sorry, you've misunderstood. You're still classed as having high blood pressure and high cholesterol regardless of the fact that the medication has lowered the levels to that classed as a normal measurement.'

'Oh!' was commonly the patient's only response.

This next incident left me asking myself the question, *'If I was to shake the patient's head from side to side, would I hear his brain rattle?!'* Allow me to explain.

My crewmate and I were dispatched to attend to a twenty-one year old male complaining of abdominal pain. Upon arriving outside of the block of flats where he lived, he was stood on the doorstep of the main entrance, waiting for us. So I invited him to step into the saloon of the ambulance and asked him to lay semi-recumbent on the stretcher.

With the young man sitting comfortably on the stretcher, I introduced my crewmate and I, and established that my patient's name was Mike. I then began questioning him about his symptoms, the time of the onset of pain, where exactly in the abdomen the pain was, etcetera, etcetera. Meanwhile, my crewmate undertook some baseline clinical observations. Following my questioning, and the completion of my crewmate analysing the patient's vital signs, I explained to Mike that in my professional opinion I didn't believe he had anything to worry about, though I still recommended that he be examined by a doctor. He accepted my professional opinion, and so consented to a visit to A&E.

During the journey to hospital, I began documenting my clinical findings, the patient's clinical observations, pain score and so on, onto my Patient Report Form (PRF), occasionally raising my head and directing my eyes at him to ask him a question and/or converse with him. That questioning and conversation went something like this:

'So, Mike, do you have any allergies to any prescription medication, at all?' I asked.

'Yeah, nuts and shellfish,' he replied.

26

For a brief moment, I just stared at him in disbelief at the answer he'd just given and thought to myself, 'What a plonker!' but instead said, 'Nuts and shellfish aren't prescription medications, Mike.'

'Oh. No then,' he replied. So I recorded NKMA on the PRF, which is an abbreviation for *No Known Medicine Allergies*. I continued completing pertinent parts of the PRF and then came to the next of kin section.

'Who's your next of kin, Mike?' I asked, not wanting to assume it was his parents. You'd be surprised at how many youngsters have no contact with their parents and, therefore, do not want them recorded as their next of kin.

'What do you mean?' he asked, looking worryingly baffled by my question.

'Well, for example, my wife is my next of kin,' I stated to assist him, and hoping it would prompt an accurate answer.

'I'm not married,' he replied. Raising my eyebrows, I stared at him, briefly stunned by his answer, before replying with,

'No, no, you've misunderstood, Mike. What I mean is…' I said, pausing to think how can I put it. 'Ah, who's your closest living relative, Mike?' I asked, hoping to simplify the matter.

'Oh, erm… my Nan,' he said with certainty.

'Your Nan?' I responded, a little surprised and looking for a nod or other sign of confirmation. 'That's unusual. Are your parents no longer alive?' I reluctantly asked, fearing they may be deceased but taking the chance as he was only twenty-one years old.

'Yeah, they're still alive,' he replied. 'But my Nan lives just around the corner from my flat. My parents live down south, so my Nan is my closest living relative,' he answered.

I was beginning to despair but found the professional strength to continue.

'OK, Mike, let me put it another way. Who would you want a

27

doctor or a nurse to contact in the event of an emergency?' I asked.

'An emergency! But you said you didn't think there was anything to worry about, that I was OK and that!' he said in a hurried, worried tone of voice.

'No, no, there isn't anything to worry about. It's normal procedure to document these things,' I emphasised to calm and reassure him.

'Oh, in that case my parents. They live in Kent, several hours' drive away. Do you want their phone numbers?'

'Yeah, go on then,' I said, thankful that I'd finally established his next of kin.

'Their landline number is five-six-two-one-nine-one. Or is it five-two-six-one-one-nine?' he said, glancing down at the floor, pondering. 'Yep, it's definitely five-two-six-one-one-nine.' I sat, rubbing my forehead in mild despair, before I said,

'That's great, Mike, but without the area code it's about as useful as a glass hammer, mate!'

'Oh, sorry, I can't remember that. I only contact them by mobile. Do you want my mum's mobile number?'

'Yeah, that'd be great, mate,' I said in a tone that, despite my best effort, was probably by now becoming unavoidably that of a fast despairing paramedic. After documenting his mum's mobile number and completing other pertinent parts of the form, I said,

'Now, moving on. Out of curiosity, have you been in Saint Winnie's Hospital before?' I asked, so I could establish whether his details would be on 'the system' or not.

'Yeah, two weeks ago,' he replied.

'Oh, right. Did you have the same abdominal pain two weeks ago then, or did you go into hospital for another reason?' I asked with significance.

'Another reason,' he said, but failed to state that reason. I waited for a moment, looking at him, hoping that would prompt him to state the reason… It didn't, so more than a little exasperated by now I asked,

'What were you in hospital two weeks ago for, Mike?' He thought about it for a second and then said,

'I was visiting my Nan. You know, the one that lives around the corner from me.'

All I could do was stare blankly down at the completed PRF. There was no *suitable* answer to that, it left me speechless and I was, therefore, relieved to arrive at the hospital a short time later, and get shut of the prize plonker!

An Eerie Encounter

It's normal Ambulance Service procedure to remove a deceased patient from a public place where death is confirmed on scene; with the exception of an instruction from the police to leave the body undisturbed if they're treating the cause of death as suspicious. That said, paramedics wouldn't cease CPR if there is a chance of reviving a patient, even in a situation where foul play is suspected and removal of the body and conveying to hospital might potentially contaminate the scene. The following incident involved an ambulance crew removing an elderly man from the street where he had collapsed in cardiac arrest one dark, late evening.

The man was confirmed dead at the scene, since he had clearly died a considerable time prior to being found, and the ambulance crew could do nothing for him… not without a heating lamp and some serious smelling salts! So, with the ambulance parked up on the roadside, the crew liaised with a police officer, who gave them authorisation to remove the body from the pavement where the deceased lay. They placed a body bag onto the ground and then, between the two of them, they carefully lifted the patient inside and zipped it up. Then, with the assistance of the police officer, they lifted the body bag onto the stretcher. The stretcher was then wheeled into the ambulance and secured in place, before the saloon lights were switched out and the rear doors slammed shut.

Leaving the scene, the crew trundled along towards the hospital mortuary, chatting away. Both the saloon and cab of the ambulance were in darkness, interrupted only by the dashboard lighting. Suddenly, while ambling along, the saloon lights came on behind them as if automatically. Startled, the paramedic sat in the attendant's seat quickly looked over her shoulder to view the back of the ambulance. Now stop that thought, I know what you're thinking but no; the deceased obviously still lay motionless in the body bag. Her crewmate, while also taken aback by the eerie event, kept his concentration on the road ahead. The attendant looked down at the lighting panel to find the switch turned to the off position. With the hairs by now standing up on the back of her neck, she flicked the switch on, and then off again, and the saloon lights went out.

Feeling spooked, they continued to drive in the direction of the hospital. Then, all of a sudden, the saloon lights came on once again.

'Is that you messing about?!' she asked her crewmate driving.

'No, is it hell, I've got both hands on the steering wheel, how can I switch the lights on?!'

'Brrrrrr, it's freaking me out now,' she said, shivering. Once again, she flicked the switch on, and then off again, and the lights went out. The driver continued to amble along the highway. A minute or so later, spookily, the saloon lights came on yet again.

'Oh, for ffff! Are you winding me up?!' she asked her crewmate.

'No, I've got both hands on the steering wheel! Just leave the saloon lights on,' he suggested.

'Yeah, OK,' she replied, flicking the light switch to on, then off and then on again, causing the saloon of the ambulance to be artificially lit for the remainder of the journey; well, I say remainder of the journey, what I mean is until they arrived at the entrance of the hospital, because just as they arrived on the grounds of the hospital, the saloon lights suddenly went out without a button being pressed by either of the crew.

'You've got to be kidding me!' she said. 'Let's get this effing body out of here now! It's giving me the bloody creeps!'

When they arrived at the mortuary, they vacated their seats, opened the rear doors, wheeled the stretcher from the ambulance and proceeded inside the mortuary. There they transferred the patient into a mortuary drawer, assisted by a porter who had been asked to meet them with a key to the building. Then they swiftly vacated the premises.

Relieved that the patient was no longer in the back of the ambulance, they cleared with ambulance control and were instructed to return to the ambulance station. Throughout their entire twenty minute journey back to base, with both the cab and saloon in darkness, the saloon lights never came back on once. Creepy, hey!

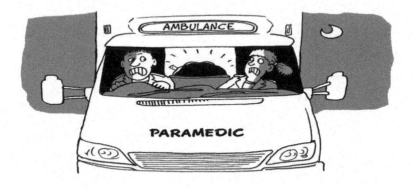

Siesta

John, a friend and former colleague of mine, was on a day shift one very hot summer's day, driving back from the A&E department to the ambulance station. His crewmate was reading the newspaper in the attendant's seat. They were comfortably ambling along when they stumbled upon a traffic jam on a long, straight road. It was so congested that John turned the engine off; they were going nowhere.

An hour went by and John's crewmate was all of a sudden startled at the sound of periodic car horns. He then realised he'd nodded off while reading the newspaper, due to the scorching temperature and lack of any breeze entering the cab. Still stationary, he looked ahead and noticed there was no longer congested traffic. He turned to ask John, sat in the driver's seat, why they were still stationary even though the traffic was no longer jammed… only to find John fast asleep too!

For about ten minutes, motorists had been driving around them, beeping their horns at John's thoughtless and inconsiderate parking in the left-hand lane of a busy road. Fantastic!

35

Recovery

An ambulance crew's vehicle had broken down while driving along the dual carriageway en route to a treble-nine call, but had managed to pull over onto the hard shoulder. They immediately informed the control room dispatcher of their predicament in order to prompt them to dispatch another crew to the incident and avoid, as much as possible, any delay to the patient. Acknowledging the message, the dispatcher informed the crew that she would arrange for the recovery vehicle to mobilise toward their location. 'Excellent,' they thought. So they gave the dispatcher their location and sat waiting patiently, having a discussion with one another.

Fifteen minutes went by and there was still no sign of the recovery vehicle, the delay prompting them to get back in touch with the dispatcher via the cab radio.

'Go ahead, over,' the dispatcher said.

'Yeah, roger. Can we have an ETA on the recovery vehicle, please? It's still not here, and I'm absolutely busting for a wee, over.'

'He's en route to you from his base,' the dispatcher said.

'Excellent, thank you,' the paramedic replied, but still a little confused as to why it was taking so long, as the location where the recovery truck was based was only several minutes' drive away from where they had broken down. A further fifteen minutes passed and there was still no sign of the cavalry. Frustrated and beginning to panic a little at the thought of peeing in his pants, the paramedic contacted the dispatcher again.

'Go ahead, over,' the dispatcher said.

'Roger, we've been sat here for half an hour, waiting. Where the hell is the recovery truck?'

'Standby, I'll get in touch with them,' she replied. The frustrated paramedic began to squeeze his own 'private parts' and rock back and forth in his seat, attempting to distract himself from the blissful thought of urinary release. Then, five minutes later - which felt more like an hour to the anxious paramedic - the dispatcher was back on the radio. 'Roger, the recovery truck has been up and down the carriageway and said he can't find you, over.'

'Well, we're on the hard shoulder, he can't miss us! And I won't miss him when I pee up his leg for making me wait so long to use the loo!' exclaimed the by now mildly frantic paramedic.

'Roger, understood. I'll get back onto them,' she replied. A further ten minutes went by and the crew were becoming increasingly irritable… and the paramedic was fast approaching his only option of peeing up the side of the ambulance in full public view! Then the radio sounded.

'Roger, the recovery man said he's been up and down the carriageway and back again and still can't find you. Where are you?' she asked.

'Where are we?! Where are we?!' he repeated to the dispatcher in disbelief before saying, in a sarcastic manner, 'Listen love, tell him we're on the hard shoulder, in a big yellow van the size of a motorhome, only one without a loo. And it has the word 'Ambulance' written across the front with green chequers, and very pretty blue lights on the roof. I'll even make them flash if it helps him, which is what I'm going to have to do in a minute if I don't empty my bloody bladder. And more to the point, if he can't see us in this then he shouldn't be bloody well driving a recovery truck anyway!'

After waiting a further twenty minutes, the crew were eventually located by the recovery vehicle. It turned out the driver had been going up and down the wrong carriageway all along. Nevertheless, the paramedic did get to use the loo before any embarrassing incontinent accidents occurred, or before he had to resort to flashing his 'meat and two veg' and peeing up the side of the ambulance in full view of the passing motorists.

Damn Velcro

Over the years, ambulance personnel's uniform has had several changes of style and manufacturer. There was a time when uniform shirts had Velcro across the top pockets, and you could have your name and job title embroidered into a cloth badge that had Velcro on the back of it; the badges could therefore be removed before putting your shirt into the wash. In my opinion, Velcro is one of the best inventions ever thought of... although its sticking-two-things-together effect can occasionally cause problems.

Case in point: My friend, Geoff, and his crewmate attended to an elderly lady who, following assessment, needed admitting to hospital. They'd assisted her onto the carry-chair in order to lift her down a flight of stairs. Geoff held the top end of the chair while his crewmate held the bottom end.

At the time of this incident, Geoff's pocket had a strip of Velcro sewn onto it, but he'd forgotten to attach his name badge onto his clean shirt. While lifting the old lady down the stairs, with her sat upright, part of her wig became stuck to the Velcro strip. As they slowly and carefully stepped down each stair, the old lady's wig began to ease gradually backwards off her head and onto Geoff's shirt pocket!

The confused old lady was completely unaware of what was happening to her wig as they were descending the stairs. Unable to stop and let go of the chair mid-way down, Geoff had no choice but to let the wig be pulled further and further from the old lady's head with each step, while chuckling to himself and fighting to keep a strong grip of the carry-chair. By the time they got to the bottom of the stairs, the wig was entirely attached to Geoff's pocket, and all he could see was the now almost bald head of the old lady.

Unable to contain themselves, Geoff and his crewmate had to finally laugh out loud then compose themselves and explain to the old lady that her wig had become detached, respectfully asking her if she would care to put it back into its correct position.

Yoo Hoo!

When I joined the ambulance service, the majority of employees, including myself, had started their careers in the Patient Transport Service (PTS), before progressing to frontline emergency duties.

A former colleague of mine was working solo on a day shift on the PTS and had completed his duties – that is, he had dropped off all of his patients back to their homes – and so drove toward the ambulance station to clock-off. Upon arriving back at base, he pulled into the parking area of the station, drove around to the rear of the garage and vacated the driver's seat in order to manually open the large, concertina-style garage doors. Then he sat himself back in the driver's seat and drove into the garage, leaving the vehicle facing the closed, similarly styled doors on the opposite side, ready for his shift the following day. He closed the rear garage doors behind him, causing the light inside to diminish considerably. He was just about to leave when he heard a softly spoken voice emerge from somewhere.

'Hellooo… Yoo hoo,' the voice said.

'Where's that coming from?' he whispered to himself. Then he heard it again.

'Yoo hoo… Hellooo… Is anybody there?' Scratching his head in confusion, he began to search around the several ambulances that were parked in the garage, wondering if one of the lads was winding him up.

'Hellooo… Hellooo… Yoo hoo. Is anybody there?' he heard once again.

'Who is that?!' he shouted.

'It's me, love, I'm in the ambulance. Can you take me home, please?' a softly spoken voice said. Gazing through the window into the back of his own ambulance, he found a little, frail old lady the size of Yoda, sat waiting patiently in her seat. She was so petite that her head was barely visible.

43

The driver apologised profusely to the little old dear and promptly drove her home.

Wrong Number

I was once passed an emergency call when, on arriving on the correct estate given to me by ambulance control, I mistakenly knocked at what I eventually discovered was the wrong address. When the occupant opened the door, looking rather puzzled as to why a paramedic was on his front step, I said,

'You did ring for an ambulance, didn't you?'

'Two years ago, yeah,' he said, with a confused expression on his face.

'Well I apologise for the delay, sir, but we have been exceptionally busy,' I replied.

Gross Misconduct

While employed by the NHS Patient Transport Service (PTS), it was common, with time served and experience, to be assigned a specific duty; for example, the 'dialysis run'. That is, several times a week you would pick up patients who required renal dialysis. You would get to know all of your patients and what particular order, from a geographical point of view, it was most appropriate to pick them up from their home addresses.

When the usual ambulance driver was on annual leave, the renal dialysis patients obviously still needed conveying to their appointments and transporting back home again. Therefore, an alternative member of staff would be assigned that duty for the week or two. This next incident, which occurred many, many years ago, involves just that circumstance of a driver covering for the regular PTS ambulance man.

So for the two weeks of his holiday, another member of PTS had been assigned his 'line', so to speak. Fast forward two weeks, and the usual driver has returned from his holiday and arrives at the ambulance station for his first day back on the 'dialysis run'.

Soon back into the old routine, he's carried out his necessary vehicle checks. He has the list of patients' names and addresses; not that he needs them, as he's on first name terms with them all and knows off by heart where they live and what order he picks them up. It's second nature to him. So off he trundles in his non-emergency ambulance, and it's not long before he arrives at his first patient's address. The gentleman ambles out of his house, quite capably, toward the awaiting 'minibus'.

'Good morning, Harold,' the driver said to his very familiar patient.

'Good morning,' Harold replied, and at the same time he takes hold of the driver's hand, turns it palm facing upwards and places an item into his hand, then steps onto the vehicle before the driver has a chance to say anything.

Staring down at his open palm, the driver is perplexed at what he sees there, but although he feels uncomfortable about it, he decides to say nothing.

The driver then moves on to his second pick-up address. This time an elderly lady trundles out of her house, down the garden pathway toward the open door of the awaiting ambulance.

'Good morning, Doris, how are you today?' he asked politely.

'Good morning, I'm fine thanks,' she replied, handing him a 'tip' in the form of two one pound coins.

Puzzled once again, but thinking that Doris and Harold must have really missed him while he was away and were now showing their gratitude and appreciation, he again chose to say nothing, feeling a little embarrassed, and instead commenced the journey to the address of his third pick-up. 'Perhaps it had been something they'd agreed to do while he'd been on his annual leave,' he thought.

Upon arriving at the address, beginning to feel quite touched by the kind gestures of appreciation, he parked up on the roadside, vacated the driving seat, opened the rear doors and lowered the ramp for his next patient. After waiting a moment, along comes Malcolm in his wheelchair, being pushed along by his wife.

'Good morning, Malcolm, have you missed me?' he asked jokingly.

'I have, yes,' he replied, while placing two one pound coins into the driver's hand. 'But I can't say I'm happy about being charged for a service that's been free on the NHS for years.'

It took a second or two for the driver to digest Malcolm's words, but then, alarmed by his comment, he quickly steps onto the vehicle. Alternating his gaze between Harold and Doris, he asked, hesitatingly at first,

'Did you two... give me that money as a tip in good gesture... or did you give it to me as some sort of fare?'

'A fare,' replied Harold in a tone that suggested it was quite normal.

'Yes, a fare,' Doris said, almost in sync with Harold. 'The driver that has been taking us for the last two weeks told us that the NHS has introduced a charge. It's going to cost us all a fortune!'

'He did what?!' the astonished driver yelled, only to have it all confirmed by the disgruntled Malcolm.

Devastated by what he had learned, the driver had no choice but to report the matter to his manager. The unscrupulous PTS staff member, who'd made a small fortune over the previous two weeks, was dismissed from the Ambulance Service for Gross Misconduct... or would Gross Mis-conducting be more fitting?!

It hopefully goes without saying that all of the patients were fully reimbursed by the Ambulance Service.

Red-Faced

An ambulance was arranged by a GP to convey an elderly patient to hospital for a routine out-patient appointment. Upon the crew arriving at the patient's address, they advanced down the garden pathway toward the front door. As the paramedic approached the front door, he began to introduce himself to a lady, the patient's wife, who was stood outside awaiting their arrival.

'Hello, my name is—'

'You'll need a chair!' she interrupted, using an abrupt tone.

Due to the lady's lack of manners, the paramedic, with his arm extended out in front of him and palm facing her as if to say 'let me stop you right there', said in an empowered and authoritative manner,

'Let me be the judge of that, Madam.'

'Well, he's got no legs!' she firmly replied. The paramedic, rather red-faced and wanting the ground to open up and swallow him whole, turned to his crewmate who was stood close by, understandably cringing, and said,

'Get us the chair and two blankets, will you mate,' before proceeding to the patient's bedroom. There he found a double amputee resting on the bed, and two prosthetic legs propped up against the wall.

OK, with a barely suppressed smile on my face, I'll reluctantly concede that in that particular case a chair was obviously required, that is, presumably the patient was unable to attach his prosthetic legs and walk. There must have been a reason why he couldn't; maybe he had an appointment at the prosthetics clinic. That's the trouble with some anecdotes, they leave you pondering on things. But anyway, if I'd been given a pound for every time a patient's relative had said to me 'you'll need a chair', not necessarily in an abrupt tone but before I've even assessed the patient's condition or mobility, well, let's just say I'd be financially better off than I am

51

right now.

Face Off

If you've ever done a First Aid course then you will probably have used a Resusci-Annie mannequin, or something similar, to practise CPR on. But, in case you haven't, a Resusci-Annie is a head and torso made from plastic and non-latex rubber. For hygiene purposes, various parts, including the face, can be removed and replaced with new parts. Resusci-Annie mannequins, amongst more highly advanced training mannequins, are frequently found on ambulance stations for self-practise and refresher training purposes. On the other hand, they've also been used to carry out numerous pranks on ambulance personnel.

For example, a member of staff got the fright of their life when they opened the door of a small cupboard room and found a life-size mannequin dressed in a paramedic's uniform... hanging. Sick and twisted you may think, but that is tame compared to much of what goes on in the ambulance service.

Now, in most ambulance stations there are armchairs for staff to relax on during downtime... though there's very little of that in today's NHS Ambulance Service! Anyway, in the early hours of one morning during a nightshift, a paramedic took a Resusci-Annie and placed it on an armchair, along with a pillow and a bunch of blankets to pad it out a little, then threw a blanket over the lot. That was done to mimic a member of staff huddled up in a foetal position on the armchair, resting. The prankster then switched the mess room lights out, so it was almost pitch black.

Upon Carla, a paramedic, returning from a treble-nine call, she immediately noticed the mannequin's plastic face popping up from beneath the blanket, even though it was dark, and removed the training dummy along with the excess blankets. She was not remotely spooked by the poor attempt at frightening her. What she didn't know was that the very plan was for her to recognise that it was a mannequin. A short time later, upon the prankster's return from a call, he found Carla had gone back out on a treble-nine call herself once again, so he set about implementing the second part of his prank.

When Carla returned to the darkened mess room, she once again noticed the mannequin's plastic face popping up from beneath the blanket, so she immediately went to pull it off the chair for a second time. But, as she grabbed the blanket, the prankster shot up from the armchair and screamed out loud. Naturally expecting it to be a Resusci-Annie and not a fellow paramedic wearing a dummy's face mask, Carla let out an almighty scream too, and ran swiftly to the ladies to change her underwear!

The Good Samaritan

My crewmate and I were dispatched to attend a two vehicle Road Traffic Collision (RTC) on a main road that had a 40MPH speed limit. We were informed by the ambulance dispatcher that there were two casualties, one in each vehicle, and that another crew would be dispatched as soon as one became available.

Being the first of the emergency services to arrive on scene, it became apparent that both casualties had vacated their vehicles prior to our arrival. One was stood on the roadside looking a little shaken; the other was sat in the front passenger seat of an uninvolved motorist's Mercedes-Benz. The Good Samaritan had stopped after witnessing the collision. So my crewmate went over to the patient who appeared unhurt but shaken. Meanwhile, I went and questioned the patient sat in the Mercedes.

'Hello, my name's Andy. What's your name, sir?' I asked.

'Tom,' he replied. I then looked at the owner of the car – the Good Samaritan – and asked,

'Can you please explain what you witnessed, sir?'

'Certainly, ole boy,' replied the well-spoken owner. 'The gentleman over there,' he said, pointing over to where my crewmate was stood talking to the other casualty, 'collided with the front of this chap's car after he pulled out of the junction, so one stopped to help, as it looked a frightfully awful crash,' he explained.

'And then what?' I asked.

'Well, this poor fellow was shaken, so I asked him if he would like to come and sit in my car. You know, to remove him from such a ghastly situation.'

'Mmm,' I murmured, while looking down the road at the two vehicles. Despite the fact that he didn't appear to have any obvious life-threatening or time-critical features, the crumple damage was significant enough to warrant my patient having a visit to the A&E for x-rays and periodic monitoring at the very least. Meanwhile, I had to determine whether he was experiencing any significant symptoms.

'Tom, please answer yes or no. Don't nod or shake your head, OK? Were you wearing your seatbelt, and did your airbag deploy?'

'Yes,' he replied, *nodding his head*. Doh! I've said that to countless patients at the scene of an RTC over the years and I can't think of one that hasn't nodded or shaken their head after I've asked them not to. Natural reaction, I guess! Anyway, I then asked,

'Tom, do you have any pain in your neck when I press on it?' looking for a response as I pressed my index finger against each of the seven cervical vertebrae in his neck.

'Yeah, that hurts,' he said, grimacing.

'Mmm,' I hummed with concern. I began considering the best course of action. In less than a minute I'd made my decision, coincidently just as the Traffic Police and Fire Service were arriving on scene. The fire officer ambled over to me. Out of earshot of everyone else on scene, I explained to him the events leading up to my patient being sat in the undamaged, uninvolved car, and the symptoms he was now experiencing. And, no surprise to me, the fire officer's reply was,

'Tut, tut, tut. What a bloody shame!'

You may think that was an odd response, though of course it was a shame Tom had been involved in an accident, but that wasn't the issue. So while the fire officer ambled back over to his crew to give them instructions, I went and explained to the 'jolly good fellow' that, although his very kind and good intention had been extremely noble of him, it was going to prove a very, very costly mistake.

Why? Well, because it was absolutely imperative that we

completely remove the roof of his beautiful Mercedes-Benz, for which he'd probably paid in the region of £60,000+.

Now, many of you will already have understood our predicament, and if you work in the pre-hospital healthcare profession then you will certainly be aware of the importance of protecting the c-spine of those involved in a significant RTC, especially when they complain of neck pain; and your dark, twisted sense of humour may have caused you to have a little chuckle at the Good Samaritan's expense... as I did shortly after the incident! However, to the layperson reading this, removing the roof of his car might seem a bit harsh and unnecessary, therefore, you may not see the funny side at all. But removal of the roof was absolutely necessary in order to minimise unnecessary movement and possibly further damage to Tom's c-spine, and failure to do so – simply to prevent an expensive car from being 'written off' – might have left the patient paralysed from the neck down for the rest of his life.

When it's put into perspective, the loss of a car, even such a stunning one, isn't too significant - it can be replaced - and maybe then it's easier to see the funny side. And in addition to potentially losing my professional registration, I wasn't prepared to take a risk that might have landed me in court, explaining to the coroner that Tom was paralysed because I couldn't bring myself to remove the roof of the Good Samaritan's dazzling motor.

After I'd explained the above predicament to the owner, he was, as you can imagine, absolutely devastated... and also extremely embarrassed that it hadn't even crossed his mind *not* to move Tom from his own crumple-damaged car.

I can just imagine what several lines of the Good Samaritan's insurance company's 'Claim Line' recorded telephone conversation transcript might have looked like.

Insurance company: 'Can you explain in detail how the crash occurred and what injuries you sustained?'

Good Samaritan: 'One was not involved in a crash, ole boy.'

Insurance Company: 'Well why is your car now a convertible then?!'

Good Samaritan: 'Ahem… well, one can explain, sir…'

I doubt they paid out, unfortunately, because insurance companies are renowned for looking for a justifiable reason not to, and I'm sure the above incident provided an ideal one! So please take heed: if you're one of those Good Samaritans that would pull over and help the occupant/s of a road traffic collision, whether you witnessed it or not, then – with the exception of the car being on fire – under no circumstances whatsoever encourage them to get out of their vehicle, or invite them to have a seat in *your* vehicle while waiting for the paramedics to arrive, even if the occupant/s have already vacated their vehicle and are walking around, seemingly unhurt; it may just cost you an absolute fortune. You've been warned!

Who Is That?

This next incident is actually rather sad, even tragic, but the circumstances surrounding the unfortunate outcome are somewhat humorous to the men and women in the ambulance service. I did warn you about *our* dark sense of humour but please forgive me if, after reading the following anecdote, it offends you in any way. To see the funny side of this story, you probably do need to be able to relate to what paramedics are frequently exposed to.

It was a lovely, warm summer's evening and an ambulance crew were just a couple of hours into their twelve hour nightshift. Now, let me quickly paint a picture in your mind's eye. The view from the station's mess room window was a woodland area that also contained overgrown foliage. The entire area was fenced off with railings that prevented anyone from entering the grounds of the ambulance station, or at least, not without some athletic ability and a fair degree of effort anyway. On this particular humid night, the crew were relaxing with the windows open, allowing a breeze to flow in, to keep them cool. In the not too distant background, the crew heard a soft sound of someone struggling to shout what they thought sounded like '*help*', but it was incomprehensible. One of the crew immediately turned down the volume on the TV, before both of them came to their feet from their armchairs and peered out through the window.

'Who was that?' one paramedic asked the other.

'Dunno,' he replied, before they both sat back down again.

'Help, awk, help, awk,' the muffled voice choked out. Sat in his armchair, one of the paramedics said,

'Who is that?' before standing and taking a second look through the window. 'There's nobody there. Where's it coming from?'

'Help, awk, awk,' the vague voice choked out once again, all but incomprehensibly.

'There it is again. Should we go and have a look and see if there's

59

anyone around?' he asked his crewmate.

'No… no, it's probably kids fooling about in the woods,' he assured his colleague. The crew were then called out on a treble-nine call and, upon their return several hours later, the window still ajar, the barely audible cries for help had ceased.

The following morning, the relieving day crew were dispatched to the woodland area. A couple of kids playing in the woods had found a body hanging from a tree. Traumatised by their experience, they had run home and raised the alarm.

It turned out that the incomprehensible, barely audible cries for help the previous night were from a suicidal man. It seems he must have changed his mind about taking his own life. After using the 'short drop' method of hanging, he didn't die immediately but was unable to remove the noose by himself and subsequently died of asphyxiation. He hadn't been able to get the attention of anybody to cut him down or raise the alarm, including the two highly trained paramedics that were only a stone's throw away from him when he jumped. Oops.

The Chase

Before you read this, I suggest that you mentally recall 'The Benny Hill Show' theme tune – or Yakety Sax by Homer 'Boots' Randolph III, to be precise – and play it in your head. Alternatively, if you're not of an age where it immediately comes to mind, go onto YouTube and type in 'The Benny Hill Show Theme Tune'. Listen to it because I'm sure it will add to the amusement of this story.

Picture the scene: it was about 9 p.m. one dark winter's night, and five or six ambulances were parked up diagonally in designated ambulance spaces outside of the hospital. Now, a handy function of the ambulance cab's built-in radio was that it could be used as a Tannoy; you simply pressed the button on the mic then switched the sirens on. No siren tones would be audible while the mic's button was depressed. You could then speak into the mic and the user's voice would be heard coming out of the Tannoy.

Anyway, while several ambulance crews were sat in their cabs outside the hospital, waiting to clear with ambulance control, another ambulance arrived and proceeded to reverse into a parking space. The crew had conveyed a rather difficult and incompliant drunken patient, and as a consequence had pre-emptively requested hospital security to meet them outside upon their arrival, in case the patient became disorderly. Parked up, and with the rear doors of the ambulance open, the security guards took up their positions ready to assist the crew to escort the patient into A&E. However, reluctant to go into the hospital before having a cigarette, the unkempt patient became disorderly when the crew told him he couldn't have one because they needed to book him in so he could be seen by a doctor. Unhappy with being denied a cigarette, he became verbally aggressive and so the police were requested to attend.

Within a couple of minutes, two police officers arrived and calmly approached the patient, but he backed off as they got nearer to him. They attempted to reason with him and reaffirm the paramedic's justification for not wanting him to have a smoke, but he wouldn't comply. So they warned him that if he didn't calm down and comply then he would be arrested for being drunk and disorderly. Paying no attention to their warnings of arrest, he became verbally aggressive with them too.

Due to his behaviour, they continued to move slowly towards him, but he just kept backing away from them. Then, all of a sudden, he ran to the front of a parked-up ambulance. The police officers gave foot-pursuit but he just sprinted away from them again, stopping around the back of a different ambulance. Once again the police moved in after him, but he just scarpered to the front of yet another parked ambulance. Observing the 'resistance to arrest' scene being played out in front of him, a paramedic sat in the cab of his ambulance decided to have a bit of fun. Using his mobile telephone held against the cab radio mic, with Tannoy function set, he played 'The Benny Hill Show' theme tune while the police gave continuous, yet unsuccessful, chase to the drunken but surprisingly elusive patient.

Onlookers, including ambulance personnel, hospital staff and taxi drivers awaiting fares, were laughing at the comical sketch of two policemen chasing after a scruffy little drunken scrote running zigzag in between several ambulances, perfectly accompanied by the unmistakeable theme tune blaring out. You couldn't write it for a sitcom, could you?

What Are the Chances of That?!

Brian was a veteran paramedic, and a very good one, too. But he was renowned for being a bit stressy and impatient, a bit of a 'flapper', you know the type. Consequently, he was often the victim of banter. Brian was working a night shift crewed with Del, another paramedic. At about 3 a.m., while Brian and Del were parked up under the canopy of the A&E ambulance bay, Pete arrived with a patient in his ambulance. After Pete had handed his patient over to the A&E staff, he began chatting to Del in private, away from Brian who was still sat in the cab of the ambulance, dozing off.

Following their brief conversation, Del adopted his position back in the attendant's seat of the ambulance. While Pete was stood talking to Del through the wound down passenger door window, they both began making conversation with Brian, who was intermittently nodding off. Del then turned to Brian, whose eyes were closed, and said,

'Blimey Brian, imagine gettin' called to a minibus crash now on the motorway, full of children, it'd be bloody awful wouldn't it, 'cause you're knackered aren't ya?'

'It doesn't bear thinkin' about, mate,' Brian replied, with his eyes closed, arms crossed and chin on his chest.

Moments later the cab radio sounded, so Brian, startled, answered it,

'Go ahead, over.'

'Roger, RED call to a sixteen-seat minibus RTC, M-fifty-six northbound. Approximately eight children on board but exact number of casualties unknown yet, over,' the male dispatcher said over the radio, with a sense of urgency in his voice.

'Jesus Christ! What are the chances of that?!' Brian asked, shocked at the coincidence. He immediately went into a flapping frenzy, rocking back and forth in his seat, breathing rapidly, and at the same time repeatedly slapped the back of his own head from sheer anxiety and anticipation of such a potentially stressful looming emergency call. Del and Pete burst into laughter and nearly pissed themselves watching Brian panic and damn near soil his uniform.

It turned out that Del and Pete had contacted their mate in the ambulance control centre and asked him to pass Brian the fictitious motorway emergency on their signal, which was to be a text message to say that they had laid the bait, now quickly pass the coincidental call. The prank went like clockwork, and the story travelled from crew-to-crew throughout the remainder of the shift. Brilliant!

Where Are You?

My paramedic crewmate, Alan, and I were parked up on standby one lovely summer's day. After enjoying a short rest, and a little sunshine, we were dispatched to attend to an elderly lady who had fallen at home and couldn't get herself up off the floor. So we proceeded in the direction of the given road name, and arrived within several minutes.

On our arrival at the correct road, it became apparent that it was a cul-de-sac, so I stopped the ambulance and told Alan to go ahead of me with the appropriate equipment, and I would turn the ambulance round and follow him in shortly. So Alan vacated the attendant's seat, grabbed the paramedic bag from the saloon, slammed the side door shut and proceeded along the roadside pavement toward the row of huge, beautiful homes; simultaneously, I moved off from the side of the road again in order to turn the vehicle round.

After negotiating the cul-de-sac using a five point turn, I eventually parked the vehicle, vacated my seat and made my way down the garden pathway toward the address. On arriving at the front entrance, I turned the handle, opened the door and stepped inside.

'Hello!' I shouted. 'Hello!' No response. 'Mmm,' I thought. 'Alan! Which room are you in?!' But there was still no audible response. So I proceeded through the door to the left of me, which led me into the lounge. There was nobody present there either, except for a little cat sat on the sofa, staring at me.

'Alan, where are you, mate?!' Nothing! No reply from Alan or anybody else. So I took my hand portable radio from my utility belt and inputted Alan's ISSI number – that's a bit like a telephone number – to enable me to contact him directly on his hand portable radio.

'Receiving, go ahead, over,' Alan answered.

'Hiya mate. Where are you?' I asked.

'I'm with the patient, she's fine. Where are *you*, you're not still parking up, surely?'

'No, am I heck. I mean what *room* are you in?'

'Oh... erm... the master bedroom, mate,' Alan informed me. So I came back out of the lounge and made my way to the master bedroom.

'Knock, knock,' I said out loud as I opened the door and entered the rather large bedroom. Once again, no Alan, no patient. 'Where the hell are they?' I thought to myself. 'Maybe this isn't the master bedroom after all. I'll try another.' So on I went to the next bedroom.

'Knock, knock,' I said, entering the room. Yet again, no Alan, no patient! So I made my way back toward the lounge and, for the second time, contacted Alan via portable radio.

'Yep, receiving, go ahead, over,' Alan answered.

'Yeah, roger, mate. I thought you said you were in the master bedroom?'

'I am mate; upstairs, first on the left,' he informed me, though it crackled with white noise as he said it.

'Sorry mate, poor reception. Can you repeat your last, over?'

'I said I'm upstairs, first on the left,' he clarified, while I stood staring at the cat relaxing on the sofa.

'Upstairs! Are you 'avin a laugh?' I asked, perplexed by his answer.

'No, why?' he replied with a confused tone.

'Well, I don't know where *you* are but I'm stood in a bungalow!' I replied.

'A bungalow! Where the hell are you?!'

'I'm inside number thirty-two 'A',' I replied.

'No, no, the patient is in number thirty-two, not thirty-two '*A*'!' he emphasised while laughing down the radio.

'Oh shit!' I said to myself out loud, and swiftly made my way down the hallway toward the front door and vacated the address immediately. I then quickly made my way next door to join Alan and the patient. I couldn't help but think though, that if nobody was in, why the door was unlocked! We did have a giggle about the incident though, and it raised some smiles round the station mess room for some time.

Jinxed

A few weeks had gone by since Carla, a very good friend of mine, had passed her paramedic course. We were working as a double paramedic crew, which was rare, and were on a nightshift parked up on standby, waiting to be dispatched to a treble-nine call. While sat in the cab of the ambulance, conversing, the topic of 'yet to be used' paramedic skills came up.

'I've not intubated anybody pre-hospital yet, have you?' Carla asked.

'Yeah, a few times,' I replied. I'd passed my paramedic course about six months before her, so I had used the majority of 'new skills' at least once by that time, with the exception of inserting a cannula into a patient's chest to disperse air from a collapsed lung; a condition known as a tension pneumothorax. That's a mouthful, isn't it!

Carla, like all other paramedics, had intubated numerous patients in the operating theatres while on practise placement. But during pre-hospital intubation, you don't have the luxuries provided during in-hospital intubation. For example, during hospital practise placement the patient has been asked to 'starve' – unless emergency surgery is being carried out of course – so the chance of the patient vomiting is slim. The patient is also lying on an operating table four feet off the floor; these things count as luxuries to a paramedic! And if that isn't enough luxury, an Operating Department Practitioner (ODP) passes you the appropriate equipment. During pre-hospital intubation it's not so easy. You're usually knelt down on the floor, with limited space, suctioning the airway, and in most cases have to rummage through your paramedic bag for the intubation equipment.

Anyway, during our discussion the cab radio sounded.

'Go ahead, over,' I said from the driver's seat.

'Roger, RED call to the conservative club, elderly male in the gents' toilets in cardiac arrest, over,' the dispatcher said.

'Roger, going mobile, over,' I replied before I turned to Carla and said, 'What were you saying about intubation? Now's your chance to get your first pre-hospital one.'

'Shit!' she replied, apprehensive about what was to come.

Upon arriving at the location given, and subsequently inside the gents' toilets, we commenced resuscitation measures and Carla achieved her first pre-hospital intubation. She was delighted to have put her first one behind her, but any sense of satisfaction was soon muted as, sadly, the patient was later certified dead at the hospital. Upon clearing from that incident with ambulance control, we parked up on standby once again. There, our earlier discussion continued.

'Have you had to deliver a baby yet? I haven't,' she said.

'Yeah a few, but I tend to look at it as assisting the mother, 'cause they deliver themselves really, don't they?' I replied.

'Yeah, I suppose, but it's still scary though, isn't it?'

'Oh yeah, I always twitch when I get sent to a 'labour' or an imminent birth, 'cause you never know whether the baby is going to come out kickin' and screamin' or not breathing... or worst case scenario, stillborn.' Then, in the midst of this discussion, the cab radio sounded again.

'Go ahead, over,' I said.

'Roger, RED call to a twenty-four year old, imminent birth, over,' the dispatcher said.

'You are joking, aren't you?!' Carla said, before I acknowledged the dispatcher's message and mobilised to the address given. Chuckling to myself, I light-heartedly said,

'That'll teach you to talk about what you haven't done yet, won't it! I suggest you keep quiet for the rest of the night now.'

A short time later, Carla experienced her first assisted delivery, there in the patient's bedroom. After conveying the elated mother to the labour suite with her newborn for company, we cleared from the hospital. For the rest of the shift, Carla chose not to mention any more of the things she hadn't yet experienced as a newly qualified paramedic, just in case she jinxed us again!

Time-Critical

I and my former colleague and very good friend, Graham, an Emergency Care Practitioner (ECP), were sat in the ambulance station when we were asked if we could respond to an elderly male who had collapsed and was unconscious. That's it, no past medical history or any other details were given. So we adopted our agreed positions in the ambulance cab, me in the attendant's seat, and Graham began mobilising with blue lights and sirens to the given address.

Upon arriving, I grabbed the appropriate equipment from the saloon of the ambulance, and Graham and I proceeded down the driveway where we were met by a very, very distraught elderly lady, Noreen, the patient's wife. We stepped inside the hallway and were escorted by her into the lounge, where we were presented with a rather large elderly gentleman called Harry, laid flat on his back on the carpeted floor.

From the outset, Graham and I immediately suspected something sinister was occurring, as he was grey, sweaty, and clammy to the touch; three typical, textbook signs and symptoms of a *potentially* time-critical condition! The situation at this stage was anything but funny. We both knelt down beside Harry, and Graham commenced obtaining some pertinent clinical vital signs. Meanwhile, I began checking his ABCs while questioning his wife, who was sobbing her heart out with worry.

'OK my love, try not to be upset, and stay calm for me. Now can you briefly explain what happened this afternoon?' I asked, while confirming that he had a patent airway, was breathing and had a palpable pulse. He did!

'Well, he's been feeling unwell all morning, and about ten minutes ago he just slumped to the floor,' she informed me with a very concerned tone.

'When you say he's been feeling unwell, in what respect; has he complained of chest pain or shortness of breath?' I asked, as I unbuttoned the collar of his shirt up to the point where it met the V-neck part of his sweater.

'No, no, he just said he didn't feel hundred percent. He said he felt weak and nauseas. Oh god, please help him, please!' she urged, extremely distressed.

'We *are* helping him my love, don't worry,' I said, before continuing with my questioning. 'And what's his past medical history?' I asked with relevance.

'Erm... He has high blood pressure, high cholesterol, angina and he's diabetic. He takes quite a lot of medication,' she explained.

Informing me that Harry was diabetic made sense, as Graham, who had just finished undertaking a blood glucose measurement on our unresponsive, grey, sweaty and clammy patient, showed me the digital display of the glucometer; it read just nought point nine millimoles per litre of blood. That was life-threateningly low! Harry could deteriorate into cardiac arrest within minutes if we didn't swiftly intervene with life-saving measures!

With Graham and I knelt down, our backs facing the upset, panic-stricken lady sat on the arm of her sofa, I began cutting the sleeve of the left arm of Harry's sweater and shirt, to expose his arm so I could look for a suitable vein to cannulate, i.e., place a needle in his arm, leaving a clear plastic tube in place. If I could obtain IV access, I'd be able to infuse some intravenous glucose into Harry's blood and, therefore, his circulatory system. Meanwhile, Graham rummaged through the paramedic bag for the cannulation equipment. With Harry's left arm now exposed, I applied a tourniquet to assist the vein to engorge with blood, and began patting his arm, which I did for thirty seconds or so. No blue tinge appeared. 'Damn!' I thought. By now, Graham was preparing a bag of glucose for me to infuse; he was obviously confident that I'd find a suitable vein and soon obtain patent IV access.

Behind me, all we could hear was Noreen waffling on about all sorts of insignificant rubbish; completely immaterial to the predicament we, and her husband, were in. It was almost as if she had absolutely no idea how time-critical Harry's presentation was. Graham and I occasionally glanced at each other and grinned at some of the gobbledygook she was coming out with. For example, she was waffling on about how the doctor had altered one of Harry's medications from ten milligram to five milligram, and then she'd become all indecisive and say to us *'no it wasn't ten milligram to five milligram, it was five milligram to ten milligram.'* Then she'd say *'he takes a yellow blood pressure tablet and a pink tablet for cholesterol. No, no, his blood pressure and cholesterol tablets are white, not yellow. I can't remember what the yellow and pink ones are for, actually, come to think of it.'* While she was babbling on, Graham and I were busy trying to prevent Harry from deteriorating into cardiac arrest!

Anyway, with no IV access possible on Harry's left arm, I cut up the right hand sleeve of his sweater and shirt, applied the tourniquet, patted a potential site and waited for a blue tinge to appear. Nothing!

The situation was becoming increasingly tense. Graham and I looked at each other, both nodding as if to say, *'we might have to scoop and run.'* The problem was, Harry was heavy and rotund, and the logistics of getting an unconscious man of his size onto a carry-chair or stretcher wasn't going to be easy whatsoever! I pondered for a moment, but could still hear Noreen jabbering on behind us, periodically crying in distress. I raised my head to glance at Graham, and said,

'I'll tell you what, Graham, let's get his shoes and socks off and I'll see if there's a vein in one of his lower legs.' So Graham proceeded to remove said clothing and I applied the tourniquet to the lower part of Harry's left leg. Once again, I waited for a blue tinge to appear. No, nothing. Zilch! Then, just when we thought the situation couldn't get any worse, to mine and Graham's horror, Harry started convulsing, probably as a result of his blood sugar levels being less than one millimole per litre of blood (<1.0mmol/l).

To scoop and run, with a man of Harry's size, wasn't a viable option while he was convulsing. And the chances of him ceasing to convulse without glucose was minimal. We desperately needed IV access. So this time I applied the tourniquet to the lower part of his right leg, patted the surface and waited for a blue tinge to appear. Moments later, a poor excuse for a blue tinge appeared under the skin.

'OK mate, you hold his leg as still as you can while I try and get a small cannula in,' I asked Graham.

'OK gov,' he replied, taking hold of Harry's right leg. By now we were both crouched down on the floor within sniffing position of Harry's feet, concentrating on this one lifesaving opportunity at obtaining IV access. The atmosphere was tense; it was a one shot deal. If I missed this we'd have no choice but to ask for a backup crew to attend and assist us to lift Harry off the floor onto the carry-chair, wheel him into the ambulance and then use diesel to get him to hospital as quickly as possible.

My forehead was dripping with sweat. Graham was sweating from restraining Harry's leg while he was convulsing. Noreen could still be heard close by, intermittently waffling, crying and panicking. As the room echoed with sounds of her angst, I lined up the needle with the vein, angled it at forty-five degrees, and took a deep breath. 'This is it, I'm going for it,' I thought to myself. Then, just as I was about to pierce the skin, Noreen all of a sudden yelled out.

'Oh no, you haven't cut his sweater have you?! That sweater is brand new!' she shouted, having come to her feet. Following her observation and disgruntled comment, I had to abort cannulation from sheer disbelief of what I'd just heard. With our backs still facing Noreen, now sat back down on the arm of the sofa, Graham and I couldn't contain ourselves and began belly laughing, discreetly so Noreen didn't realise. Tears streamed from our eyes, and our stomachs shook with the intensity of the muted laughter. Meanwhile, Harry continued to convulse, but because Graham's grip had loosened from around Harry's leg, there was no way I could attempt cannulation; his leg was far too shaky.

After being in discreet but incapacitating fits of laughter for a

76

minute or so, Graham took hold of Harry's leg once more, and I lined up the cannula again, took a deep breath and tried to get Noreen's comment out of my head. Then all of a sudden, as if all distress, panic, grief, worry and concern had gone, she said,

'I can't believe you've cut his sweater. That cost a fortune!'

I couldn't hold back the stifled but no less debilitating need to laugh and was forced to abort cannulation once again! Graham and I broke into a further fit of heavily suppressed giggling for a second time, and tears filled my eyes to the point that my view of Harry's leg was blurred. We just couldn't stop laughing. There was no way I could attempt cannulating while laughing as much as I was.

Paramedics learn to handle and suppress all kinds of emotions while on duty, but I never expected to find myself and Graham dealing with a time-critical patient while trying to control such fits of laughter. Thankfully, because we had our backs to Noreen, she remained completely unaware that we were silently laughing so much.

In order to compose myself and get this lifesaving cannula into Harry's leg, I had to imagine something serious... such as Harry dying on me! That helped me compose myself enough to have another crack at obtaining IV access. However, just as I was about to cannulate, Harry's wife piped up again.

'That cost twenty-nine, ninety-nine, that did! Harry loves that sweater; it's his favourite one now,' she emphasised. This time, remaining composed, I turned to face her and, using an empathetic tone said,

'Noreen, your husband's experiencing a hypoglycaemic episode. His blood sugar levels are so low it's causing him to convulse. He's extremely unwell. So don't worry, it's just a sweater; a thirty quid sweater, that's all.'

'Yeah but it's brand new. He'll go mad,' she replied, absolutely certain he was going to survive this event. I looked at Graham and whispered,

'If I don't get this cannula in then he won't be alive to go mad, and she won't need to replace the sweater, anyway.' I then turned my head to face her again and replied, 'Well, if you write to the ambulance service and complain, my love, then I'm sure they'll reimburse you, OK?' I said, calmly, and doing my utmost best to hide my despair.

Talk of reimbursement did the trick, though; she made no further comments about the sweater! Fortunately, I managed to secure IV access in Harry's lower right leg and infused some diabetic juice into his circulatory system, bringing him back to a state of full consciousness. And, contrary to Noreen's perceived response to his sweater being ruined, he didn't give two hoots. He was just pleased to be alive.

Who Needs Enemies?

Communication via static and hand portable radios has evolved and improved since I joined the ambulance service in 2002. Back then, partial 'open speech' was the norm; that is, you could hear what the control room dispatcher said to a paramedic or ambulance technician, but you were unable to hear a crew member's reply to the dispatcher's instructions, message or comment. While a member of an ambulance crew spoke to the dispatcher, all you would hear were multiple 'beeps'. Following those 'beeps', all you would then hear was the dispatcher's response to what the paramedic had said.

That was the norm, but ambulance control room operators could adapt the communication so that full 'open speech' was possible, which they occasionally did. That way you could hear two-way conversations on the radio. Nowadays, communication via the radio is very discreet. Today, crews can choose to speak one-to-one with the dispatcher and nobody else can listen in to the conversation, partially or wholly. That has improved patient confidentiality considerably, because names and addresses are no longer aired over the radio for all and sundry to hear.

Being able to listen in on partial conversations proved to be quite amusing at times, because it was left to your own imagination as to what the paramedic must have said to the dispatcher to get the response heard on open speech when the dispatcher replied.

Have you ever heard of *Bob Newhart*, the American stand-up comedian and actor? Surely you've heard of the notorious *'Driving Instructor'* and *'Defusing a Bomb'* comedy sketches, haven't you? If not, you should purchase Bob's audio CD called *'Something Like This...The Bob Newhart Anthology'*. It's hilarious, and no, I'm not on commission. His comic material involves him simulating one-way conversations on the telephone, radio or sometimes as if someone is sat next to him. Bob's verbal responses to a non-visible, non-audible character he is pretending to converse with enables the audience to use their own imagination as to what the character must have said to him. I remember a particular one-way-audible radio conversation that reminded me of a typical Bob Newhart sketch: it cracked me up and made me think, with colleagues like that, who needs enemies?!

I was working solo on an RRV parked up on standby. An ambulance crew had responded to a treble-nine call and had arrived on scene in an area that I will call Scrotesville, which is a communal area where an abundance of scrotes reside. From the one-way conversation that I could hear, they were evidently experiencing problems with the patient or one or more of the patient's relatives or friends. The brief conversation went something like this.

'Ambulance Control, pass your priority,' the dispatcher said. Then all that I heard while the paramedic spoke was beep, beep, beep, beep, beep, before the dispatcher spoke again.

'Roger, understood, I'll request the police to immediately respond RED, over.' The paramedic's response was inaudible and once again all I heard was beep, beep... Then the dispatcher replied with, 'Roger, understood. Is your crewmate OK? Are you both able to leave the scene, over?'

Beep, beep, beep...

'Did you say he's been assaulted, over?' she asked in a concerned tone.

Beep, beep, beep...

'Oh god! Roger, the police are en route, but I'm also gonna dispatch another ambulance for your crewmate, over.' The dispatcher then contacts another ambulance crew and passes the following message in a fast but shaken voice: 'Roger, can you respond to outside the Halfway House; your colleagues are in danger. One of them has been assaulted; he's got head and facial injuries, possibly knocked unconscious, over.' By now I was listening quite intently to each disconnected half of the conversation coming over the radio, realising colleagues appeared to be in some distress.

Beep, beep, beep, beep, beep...

'Yes, the police are en route, over!' she said, sternly.

Beep, beep, beep, beep...

'Yes, I realise you're on your break, but it's a friend from the same station as you!'

Again, all I heard was beep, beep, beep, beep... Then, the dispatcher's reply came,

'OK, I stand corrected, he may not be a friend as such but he is your colleague, for crying out loud!'

Beep, beep, beep, beep, beep...

'I don't believe you! Anyway, understood, I'll contact you when your break is over. That is unless I get a crew available sooner,' she sternly replied.

Beep.

Well that was it, I was in stitches when I heard the dispatcher's reply, and that last stand alone beep. I could only assume that the paramedic had simply replied with,

'Roger.'

I then had visions of a paramedic eating a tasty, amply filled sandwich, not giving two-hoots that one of his fellow colleagues – not 'a friend' – from the same ambulance station had been assaulted and may have been badly injured. No, it's nowhere near as funny as Bob Newhart's sketches, but nevertheless, at the time I found it hilarious.

Bamboozled

My crewmate, Adam, and I were dispatched to attend to an elderly male patient reportedly having a stroke. On arriving inside the bungalow, I eagerly asked the treble-nine caller, the patient's wife, where her husband was. Very calmly, she informed me that he was in the bathroom. So Adam and I rushed to the bathroom situated along the hallway.

The bathroom door was closed and so, anticipating that the patient might be slumped on the other side, I slowly and carefully opened it, not wanting the door to bang against him. As I opened the door, peeking my head around it, I was shocked to find the gentleman with his face covered in shaving foam… stood having a shave!

'What the hell…?' I thought, 'That's not the typical presentation of someone having a stroke!' Baffled, I asked him to go into the lounge to have a chat as to the reasons why we were there. So, sat in the lounge with the patient and his wife, I began ascertaining some information.

'So, what's the concern here this morning?' I asked the lady.

'Well, he woke up this morning a little confused and he can't remember things from yesterday. And he was talking a bit gobbledygook, if you know what I mean?'

'Mmm,' I responded with a nod. 'And in your opinion is he back to normal now?'

'Yes, sort of.'

'OK, good.'

Adam and I then undertook some thorough further questioning and observations. While doing so, his wife informed us that they were supposed to be going to Buckinghamshire that day – which was over one hundred miles away from their address – to visit their son, but had now decided against it. She chose to telephone her son in our presence to let him know, and that telephone conversation went something like this.

'Hiya, love, I've got the paramedics here at the moment. Your dad took a funny turn this morning.' She paused while her son spoke and then said, 'Yeah, we're not gonna come now Son, not while he's been funny.' A brief pause came again. Then she said, 'I don't know what they're gonna do with him yet, they've not said because they're still doing tests on him.' At that point, while Adam and I were crouched alongside each other continuing to assess the patient, I whispered to her,

'Do you want me to talk to him and explain things clearer?'

'Hang on Son, the paramedic's saying something,' she said, before covering the telephone receiver with her hand. 'What did you say, my love?' she asked me.

'I said do you want me to talk to him and explain things clearer?'

'You can't, love, he's miles away, in Buckinghamshire,' she replied, before carrying on talking to her son. Adam and I just looked at each other, our jaws on the floor, bamboozled by her reply.

'Did I just hear right then, that I can't speak to him because he's in Buckinghamshire? What the hell difference does that make, he's on the telephone?!' I whispered to Adam, with a huge grin on my face.

She never did pass me the telephone to speak to her son, and so I didn't get the chance to explain to him what my clinical impression of his dad was. Every so often throughout the rest of the shift, Adam and I would chuckle to ourselves recalling the sweet old lady's illogical comment.

The Irony

In the UK, excessive alcohol consumption is on the increase amongst the young and not so young in today's society. Paramedics are renowned for frequently attending to people experiencing the effects of being under the influence of alcohol; whether it is in the street, a police cell or in their own home.

I remember my crewmate, Lisa, a paramedic, and I being dispatched to an address in the early hours of the morning during a night shift, to attend to a fifty-odd year old man who had rung treble-nine stating that he needed help with his addiction to alcohol. There's very little a paramedic can do for alcoholism, but we do attend to such people a lot... an awful lot! Anyway, upon arriving inside the treble-nine caller's lounge, it became apparent that he was living in sub-standard conditions – from my experience, alcohol addiction was probably a contributing factor. The floor of his uncarpeted lounge was strewn with no less than one hundred (and that's no exaggeration!) empty cans of high-strength lager. So, stood facing our patient, who was sat on his sofa, I began by introducing Lisa and I.

'Good morning, my name is Andy and that's Lisa,' I said, pointing to my crewmate. 'What's your name?' With slurred speech he replied,

'Mick.'

'Nice to meet you, Mick, what's your concern at this ungodly hour?' I asked.

'I'm an alcoholic,' he replied, with a sad, sombre facial expression.

'Is that the main reason you've called us, or is there another reason, too?' I asked.

'No, that's it. I'm an alcoholic, and I need help now, 'cause the doctor said if I don't stop drinking then I'll be dead in six months,' he explained.

'Really, the doctor told you that straight up, did they?' I asked.

'Yeah,' Mick said. 'Straight up, no bullshitting me. He said Mick, if you don't stop drinking, you'll be dead in six months or less.'

'OK. Did the doctor discuss options with you, such as admitting you to a specialist residential clinic? It lasts about three or four weeks, I think. It's proved to be successful for some alcoholics,' I explained empathetically, in an encouraging and positive manner. Mick then tittered to himself, glanced at me and Lisa, and with a raspy, rattling smoker's cough said,

'Yeah, he did. Thing is, there's a twelve month waiting list!'

Dumbfounded by Mick's comment, Lisa and I – who both possess a very dark sense of humour – couldn't hold back, and subsequently burst into a fit of nervous laughter. After a short time, we composed ourselves, and I then said to Mick,

'I don't know what to say, Mick. I'm speechless!' Mick, on the other hand, continued laughing and popped the ring pull of another can, and then casually said,

'It's ironic, isn't it? Six months to live, but a twelve month waiting list for treatment to stop me from drinking. I'm screwed, so I might as well 'ave another drink, 'adn't I!'

Mick's horizontal attitude to his predicament prompted more laughter from me and Lisa. But later, despite the politics and bureaucracy involved in alcoholics receiving treatment at the residential clinic in question at the time of this incident, I did put a referral in place to try to get Mick admitted as soon as possible.

Frequent Encounters

There are two things guaranteed in life: death and taxes. Now, I wasn't counting but I imagine I attended to and pronounced at least one thousand people dead during my career. Pronouncing that someone is dead is a frequent encounter for ambulance personnel and, with the exception of children and young adults, you get used to it: it may sound heartless to the layman but it becomes like water off a duck's back, particularly when the patient is elderly. However, what may or may not surprise you is that people don't just die of natural causes while fast asleep in bed. Oh no. Paramedics often attend to deceased patients and find them in the most bizarre positions.

I once attended to an elderly lady who was in her bedroom, sat on a commode that was flush against a wall. She had died while emptying her bowels. I can only assume it was a relief for her, because I found her as stiff as a board, with her eyes wide open and a huge grin on her face. I imagine she must have strained for a little while before inducing any movement, and the straining had caused her to have a massive, instantaneous, fatal heart attack after she'd passed a motion.

On another occasion, a close friend of mine attended to an old lady whose neighbour had called the ambulance service out of concern for the elderly person next door; it was late on in the afternoon and she noticed milk still stood on the lady's doorstep, which was unusual for her. On his arrival, approaching her from behind, he found her sat on a dining chair with one leg crossed over the other, leaning forward, with her right forearm resting on her leg, and her left hand under her chin, as if pondering over something. When he proceeded further towards the lady, he wasn't sure whether she was dead or whether she'd not heard him entering her house. So, not wanting to startle her, he whispered,

'Hello... hello, it's the paramedics.' When he failed to get an answer, he went around the front of her and shook her shoulders, but rigor mortis had clearly set in. She had died while sat in a pondering position with her eyes still open.

Two other close colleagues of mine experienced a similar incident. They were dispatched to an elderly male whose neighbour was supposed to be cleaning his carpets for him. After several attempts to gain the elderly gent's attention by knocking on the front door and ringing the doorbell, but having no joy, he decided to ring treble-nine for an ambulance, as he was concerned for the gent's welfare. Upon the crew arriving and them forcing entry to the property, they were presented with a male who appeared to be sat upright on an armchair in the lounge, mid-way to pulling his sweater over his head. His face could not be seen, but he was completely motionless, like a statue.

'Is he alright?' the concerned neighbour asked the paramedic. On inspection of the patient, the paramedic replied,

'No, he's dead I'm afraid.' Sadly, the man had died while removing his sweater and rigor mortis had set in while sat in that position. It's fascinating, isn't it?!

What made that sad incident a little humorous for the attending crew who witnessed it was that the neighbour casually asked the paramedic,

'Do you think he would still want me to clean his carpets?'

You What?!

My crewmate, John, and I were on standby waiting to be dispatched to an emergency call. After a short time, the cab radio sounded.

'Go ahead, over,' I said.

'Roger, RED call to a 'tee year old, imminent birth, over,' the dispatcher said, but her message transmitted unclearly over the radio, so we looked at each other a little perplexed.

'The reception is poor, isn't it? Did she say forty year old, imminent birth then?' I asked John.

'I think so. Ask her to repeat the age again,' John said as he began mobilising to the address given, so I contacted ambulance control.

'Control, go ahead, over.'

'The reception was poor. Can you please confirm that we're attending to a forty year old, imminent birth, over?' I asked.

'No, negative, fourteen years old – one-four, fourteen years old, over,' the dispatcher confirmed.

'Fourteen?!' I shouted over the radio.

'Yep, a sign of the times I'm afraid. Good luck lads,' she said.

So we continued toward the location on blue lights, with a bucket full of anticipatory adrenaline flowing through our veins. That's quite normal when dispatched to an imminent birth, as paramedics get limited obstetric and maternity training: adrenaline hurtles through your veins because of the relative lack of knowledge of the subject matter and the effect that has on your confidence.

When we arrived, we quickly vacated our seats, grabbed the maternity equipment, amongst other appropriate kit, and hurried into the house. There we were met by a lady in her late thirties, who I correctly assumed was the patient's mum, pacing back and forth in the lounge area, appearing very angry. With no time to introduce myself, I emphasised the urgency of the matter and sternly said to the lady,

'Where's the patient?!'

'She's locked herself in the bloody bathroom. I'm gonna kill her when she gets out!' she shouted.

While John stayed with the incensed woman, I went upstairs and stood outside of the locked bathroom door. I could hear the young girl sobbing her heart out. So, gently knocking on the door, I said,

'Hello, my name's Andy, I'm a paramedic. Can you let me in so I can help you?' Without hesitation, the girl opened the door, allowing me to enter the bathroom. She immediately sat down on the floor and continued to cry. My first impression was that birth wasn't imminent at all, but she was pregnant, although she didn't overly appear to be. She was very slim and barely had a 'baby bump'. Upon questioning the young girl about her pregnancy and how far apart her contractions were, amongst other things, it became apparent to me that she had begun getting contractions while in the presence of her mum. But her mum didn't even know she was pregnant: the daughter had only confessed several minutes prior to an ambulance being called. So, attempting to console the teen, I said,

'Listen, love, your mum will come around to the idea. She's just shocked because of your age, that's all.' Still sobbing, the girl replied,

'It took ages for her to come around last time.'

'What do you mean, last time?' I asked her.

'This is my second baby. I've already got a one year old.'

'You what?!' I thought, but instead replied with, 'Ah, that explains why your mum is going mad down there, doesn't it.'

'Yeah, she's gonna kill me.' Rubbing her back to provide some reassurance, I said,

'No she won't, don't worry.'

'She will. She did last time 'cause I didn't know who the dad of

94

my first baby was,' she said, sobbing.

'You what?!' I thought once again, but instead replied with, 'Oh, right. Well she'll come around eventually, don't worry. Where's your unborn baby's dad. Have you contacted him to let him know you've been having contractions?'

'No, I can't,' she answered.

'Why not, is he at work?' I asked her. With a progressive build-up of another bout of crying, she replied,

'No, that's why she's gonna kill me... I don't know who the father is.'

'You what?!' I thought yet again, but this time I was so shocked I didn't know *what* to say.

We eventually conveyed the teen to the maternity ward, along with her mum, who did eventually calm down while en route to the hospital. The dispatcher was right though: unfortunately it is a sign of the times, especially in the UK.

What's Your Problem?!

The location of one of my many former ambulance stations was approximately two hundred yards away from the local hospital, though it was a community hospital rather than Accident and Emergency. One particular colleague and paramedic, Colin, was a little hard of hearing. No, that's an understatement; he was practically as deaf as a post. And so while he was sat in the mess room in possession of the TV remote, the volume would often be set to very loud.

One evening, while on a night shift, Colin was sat down watching TV along with several of his peers. The volume on the TV was blaring, so they were barely able to hear each other speak. When the mess room telephone rang, Colin surprisingly heard it ringing, so being the closest, he answered it.

'Hello, station,' he said.

'This is Sister Curtis. Is it absolutely necessary for you to have the television that loud? We can hear it on A1 ward. Can you please turn it down immediately!'

'Eh, you what?' he asked the sister.

'Turn your television down at once!' she said.

'What's your problem?!' Colin abruptly asked.

'My problem is the volume of your television! Now turn it down at once!' she repeated. Colin slammed the telephone down, walked out of the mess room, and descended the stairs of the ambulance station with haste.

Onlooking colleagues wondered what the hell was happening. He was about to stomp out of the door and march across the grounds of the hospital to pay a visit to the complaining sister, when Becky, another paramedic, emerged from another room. She never had a chance to say anything to Colin, he just looked at her and said,

'I'm going to the hospital! A bloody nurse just rang here

complaining about the TV volume being too loud!' Becky couldn't keep a straight face and just burst out laughing, quickly informing Colin that it was her that had rung him to wind him up over the volume of the TV. He was initially... let's just say, displeased with her, but eventually saw the funny side of the prank, especially once his peers got to hear about it and subsequently took the mickey out of him for frequently having the TV so unbearably loud.

Eats, Shoots and Leaves

Punctuation: it can change the entire meaning of a sentence. Now, I assume you've heard of 'He Eats, Shoots and Leaves'. If you remove the comma after 'Eats', you would quite conceivably think that the sentence was about a panda who eats shoots and leaves for his dinner. However, keep that comma in and the sentence might suggest a soccer player - eats something, shoots the ball at the goal and then leaves the pitch.

Another well-known example of incorrect punctuation changing the entire meaning of the sentence is 'Let's eat grandad'. Poor grandad, hey! Alternatively, it could be written: 'Let's eat, Grandad'. Now grandad isn't going to be eaten, instead he's going to have something to eat.

Now, why this reminder of the importance of punctuation? Well, before transferring back up north, a small part of my previous role down south, as a Paramedic Clinical Support Officer, involved auditing clinicians' electronic patient clinical records (ePCR) for data input. Did you spot the missing comma in the previous sentence? During my career, I never attended to an 'electronic patient'. Anyway, auditing electronic, patient clinical records was done to ensure that the correct drugs and drug dosages were documented, and that the appropriate assessments were undertaken. In addition to that, I would check that an adequate and comprehensive set of notes were recorded, amongst a lot of other clinical details too. The purpose of quarterly audits was to make sure that clinicians did not leave themselves wide open to criticism and litigation by the coroner or a solicitor who cross-examines them in the event that a disgruntled patient wishes to sue the NHS.

While undertaking a patient clinical record audit, I wasn't interested in the paramedic's understanding of the English language, and it certainly wasn't my place to provide positive or negative feedback about their spelling, grammar or punctuation. But I did occasionally come across some very funny sentences and couldn't help but chuckle to myself. Case in point: the following sentences were taken from real patients' documentation recorded by a variety of paramedics.

This first example is my favourite, and was taken from a set of notes about a patient who had an ulcer on his leg.

'Gent sat in lounge with foot up District Nurse, came to see him this a.m.'

What I think the paramedic meant was:

'Gent sat in lounge with foot up. District Nurse came to see him this a.m.'

This second example was taken from a set of notes about a patient who came close to collapsing in a supermarket store.

'The patient was stood in the queue at the supermarket for the past month. She has been periodically feeling dizzy whenever she is stood still.'

What I think the paramedic meant was:

'The patient was stood in the queue at the supermarket. For the past month she has been periodically feeling dizzy whenever she is stood still.'

Another example where misplaced punctuation changed the meaning of the sentence:

'The patient, who is 37/40 weeks pregnant, slipped on the wet kitchen floor yesterday and stated in her own words that 'her legs just slipped apart' while trying to conceive and during pregnancy, the patient had pelvic, and hip ligament problems.

What I think the paramedic meant was:

'The patient, who is 37/40 weeks pregnant, slipped on the wet kitchen floor yesterday and stated in her own words that 'her legs just slipped apart'. While trying to conceive and during pregnancy, the patient had pelvic and hip ligament problems.'

I wish I'd found a few other humorous examples while auditing paramedics' patient documentation, but unfortunately - or rather,

100

fortunately I suppose - such punctuation errors are few and far between. It's probably a good thing that errors are infrequent because a prosecuting solicitor would have a field day, I'm sure, as what is written, whether correctly or incorrectly, would be used against the health care professional to its fullest extent if financial compensation was the intended purpose for suing the NHS.

'Gent sat in lounge with foot up District Nurse'

The Golden Girls

OAPs... I love 'em, they're great, and they make up a fair majority of the treble-one and treble-nine incidents that ambulance personnel attend to, for obvious reasons. They're also the subject of many of the countless anecdotal stories that I can recall. For instance, I was called to attend to an elderly lady who had fallen at home. On my arrival, I found her lying flat on her back on the lounge floor of her bungalow, being cared for by three of her elderly friends. Together, they were like Blanche, Rose, Dorothy and Sophia, the old dears from the US sitcom, *The Golden Girls.* They were as funny as them too.

Fortunately, my patient hadn't lay there for long, as I'd been dispatched to her shortly after she'd fallen. I knelt down next to her and asked her not to move until I'd assessed her... well, *shouted* for her not to move, as she was as deaf as a post. I wanted to ensure she'd not potentially fractured the ball and socket joint of her hip bone – better known as the neck of femur – which is a common occurrence in the elderly following a fall. So I then began by ascertaining her name.

'Hello, my name's Andy, I'm a paramedic. What's your name, flower?' I asked. Straining her eyes while looking at *Blanche,* she shouted,

'What de'say?!'

'I said, what's your name?!'

'Eh, what de'say?!' she repeated. Moving a little closer to her, I said,

'What's your name, petal?!' With her nose scrunched and eyes squinting, she bellowed,

'What de'say, do I live on my own?!'

Rose, despairing, yelled,

'*Sophia,* tell him your name!'

Laughing, I said to *Rose,*

'Is her name *Sophia,* by any chance?'

'Yeah, have you been to her before?' she asked with interest.

'No, you fool, you've just called her by her name!' I said, chuckling. The Golden Girls giggled to themselves, with the exception of *Sophia;* bless her, she still didn't have a clue what we were talking or laughing about.

Unbelievable!

I attended to an elderly chap named Brian, who had fallen while stood under a bus shelter, waiting for the number five. He reminded me of *Compo* from the UK sitcom, *Last of the Summer Wine*; you know, the scruffy little sod. After a thorough check-up in the back of the ambulance to make sure he had actually fallen and not collapsed, and to ensure there were no underlying causes for the fall, I informed him that he didn't need a visit to the A&E department, which he was pleased about. Before I could let him on his way though, I had to complete the non-conveyance forms, and therefore went about ascertaining some personal details from him. Part of that conversation went something like this:

'So, your first name is Brian, is that right?' I asked, to reconfirm.

'Yes, that's right,' he answered.

'OK, is that Brian with an 'I' or a 'Y'?' I asked. He thought about it for a second and then looked at me with a confused expression,

'With a 'B',' he answered. Unbelievable! I did eventually complete my documentation and assisted Brian from the ambulance and back to the bus shelter, from where I assume he got home safely.

Zero to Ten

As you can see from the last two anecdotes, attending to old folk is often a giggle – though it can also be mildly frustrating, especially while trying to determine their perceived pain score. It's like trying to draw blood from a stone. The conversation is often similar to the following:

'So, Fred, about your abdominal pain, on a scale of zero to ten, how would you score your pain right now? Zero being no pain and ten being the worse pain you have *ever* been in.'

'Er… well, I've had worse.'

'OK, how would you score it now though, zero to ten?'

'Er… well, I fell and broke my wrist last year; that did hurt, I tell you. It's not as bad as that though.'

'Yeah, OK, but zero to ten, how is your abdominal pain?'

'Well, if I keep still, it's less painful than when I move.'

'Zero to ten, Fred, zero to ten?'

'I'm not sure really. It's probably more than a two.'

'Maybe a three then, Fred?'

'No, no, it's more than a three. Probably between four and six, I'd say.'

'Fred, should I put five down?'

'Yeah, yeah, it's about that, yeah.'

I'll say it again, old people, I love 'em, and I always had plenty of time for each one that I attended to. In fact, when a visit to the hospital wasn't required, I'd frequently stick around on scene for a short time to make them a brew and have a chat about the history of their lives. The vast majority of them had fascinating stories to tell – believe me, you'd be astonished!

Gas Man

Several years ago, prior to the implementation of the NHS treble-one service, part of my role as an NHS paramedic was to man the telephone triage desk for the GP Out-of-Hours service (OoH). This service was available on weekdays, after the GP surgeries had closed, and twenty-four hours a day on Saturday and Sunday. The role involved sitting at a desk equipped with a keyboard, two monitors and a telephone with headset, though I wouldn't always use the headset. There, I'd wait for a call taker to ascertain a caller's details and input them before passing the information on to me via the software system.

I would then open the incident detail and call the patient back, or the person calling on behalf of the patient, and upon them answering I'd introduce myself as a paramedic and thoroughly question them to determine the patient's presenting signs and symptoms, in addition to any other significant history. I'd then offer either self-care advice, arrange a GP to visit them in their home – depending on their age, mobility etcetera – or ask them to attend the clinic at a specific time; on rare occasions I'd dispatch an emergency ambulance to them.

I have to be honest, I hated it, because I much preferred to assess patients face to face, physically observing the patient's clinical presentation myself and not via the telephone, because you could only rely on the information given by the caller, and their perceived seriousness of the symptoms they were complaining of. But while it wasn't a role I enjoyed, there were occasional calls that had me and my fellow telephonists cracked up with laughter.

Now, please bear in mind, the GP out-of-hours service was implemented for people who had health concerns that could not wait until the next morning during a weekday evening or in the early hours, or until after the weekend. However, the out-of-hours service was severely abused by the general public. You'd be amazed at some of the problems that people considered needing immediate attention, for example: haemorrhoids, a stye on the eye

109

and, believe it or not, a hangover!

Case in point: this next incident occurred one sunny Saturday morning. I'd been on duty manning the GP out-of-hours service desk since 7am. Just a few hours of my shift had gone by... well, dragged by would be more accurate, and I was sat at my desk thinking 'God I'm bored! Please, please let them be short of paramedics on the road today and let me get out of here.' I'm sure I suffer from thaasophobia – the fear of being idle or bored.

Anyway, there I am, suffering from thaassophobia, when an incident pops up on the monitor. It says **Name:** *Joe Windass*. **Age:** *67.* **Clinical Concern:** *Excess Flatulence.* 'You gotta be kidding me,' I thought, double checking what appeared on the screen. 'What... and that warrants the use of the GP out-of-hours service?! Bloody hell, what's the world coming to?!' I picked up the telephone receiver and proceeded to key in 'Mr Windy-ass's' telephone number. After several rings, he answered.

'Hello,' he said. I then immediately heard a *PAAAAARP* down the telephone line, followed by a brief moment of silence before another *PAAAAARP*. I instantly bit down on my knuckles to try and stop myself from bursting into laughter.

'Hello!' he repeated, this time louder, as I'd seemingly initially ignored him. I took a deep breath and composed myself before saying,

'Hello, is that Mr Joe Windass?'

'It is, yeah. Morning, Doctor, I really need your help, I've—'

'Let me stop you there, Joe,' I said, interrupting him. 'It's not the doctor. My name is Andy; I'm a paramedic working for the GP out-of-hours service. I'm calling with regards to your concern. Can you just confirm what your concern is this morning, please?' I asked in case there was more to his problem than mere excess flatulence.

'I can't stop fartin', Doctor!' he shouted. Before I even had chance to reply to him, I heard *PAAAAARP* down the line once again, followed by another brief moment of silence and then another

110

PAAAAARP. In an attempt to contain myself from laughing uncontrollably at the sheer volume level and the length of time each emission of methane gas lasted, I clenched my fist and bit down on my knuckles once again. After a few seconds, I released my clenched fist from my mouth, took a deep breath right down from the diaphragm, and then began questioning him.

'Joe, I'm not a doctor, I'm a paramedic, OK? Now, how long have you had excess flatulence for?' I asked. He didn't answer my question straight away; the line seemed to go silent again, and then I heard, *PAAAAARP...*

'Oh god!'... *PAAAAARP... PAAAAAAARP!* 'Oh Jesus!' After several bursts of flatulence, he said, 'It only started this morning, Doctor.'

'Surely I don't have to keep telling him that I'm not a doctor,' I thought, but instead replied, 'Joe, do you have any other symptoms at all, such as persistent abdominal pain, bloating, or frequent episodes of diarrhoea or constipation?'

'Yeah, I've got the squits, Doctor. My poo's like rusty bum wee and my bum burns when I go the loo. My asshole is like a blood orange at the moment, Doctor,' he shouted, as if in distress, and also not embarrassed to tell it as it is.

'Too much information,' I thought, scrunching my nose up, before continuing to question him further. 'OK Joe, I understand you're distressed. Now, can I ask what foods you've eaten since yesterday afternoon?' I asked with relevance.

'Erm... I had a Phall curry from the Indian...' Then came a momentary pause before I heard 'Oh Jesus, hang on,' before another *PAAAAARP* resonated down the phone line. 'Oh, bloody hell.' *PAAAAARP... PAAAAARP!* 'Oh, sweet Lord, Mary Mother of Jesus. I need help, please make it stop Doctor, please,' he pleaded.

'Did you say you had a Phall curry, Joe?' I asked, to reconfirm, as that had significance.

'Yeah, a Phall. It were bloody hot it were, Doctor, and it's bloody

111

well burning me bum now!' The line went silent for a moment once again before yet another loud *PAAAAARP.... PAAAAARP... PAAAAARP* travelled down to me as if echoing. I was bent over the desk, laughing as quietly and discreetly as I could. While I was doing so, I could hear Joe's voice faintly down the line saying,

'Hello. Hello, Doctor. Are you still there?' Composing myself, with tears of laughter running down my cheeks, I eventually managed to answer.

'Sorry Joe, yes I'm still here. Sorry about that, just a slight technical issue. Now, Joe, for your information, a Phall is generally three, four, maybe even five times hotter than a Vindaloo. I'm not surprised it's burning your backside and giving you excess flatulence. Had you tried a Phall prior to last night?'

'No, never, and I won't be bloody well 'avin one again either!' he emphasised. *PAAAAARP... PAAAAARP.* 'Oh, good lord! Please help me, Doctor!' *PAAAAARP.* 'Please make it stop,' he said, pleading with me once more, as if I had some miracle cure.

I sat in my chair, bent over, with my elbows resting on the desk, intermittently holding my hand over my mouth and biting down on my knuckles, thinking why is this happening to me? I took a deep breath once again and said,

'Joe, I think you're just going to have to ride it out, and—'

'Hang on...,' he said, interrupting me ...*PAAAAARP!* 'Gordon Bennett, what the hell's up with me?! Sorry, go on Doctor, you were saying?'

'Joe, I was going to say that you'll just have to ride it out and let nature take its course.'

'Is there nothing you can do for me, Doctor? I can't cope with being like this all day,' he said.

'To be honest with you Joe, there's nothing that can, or even needs to be done today. I suggest you lay off the curries for a while, particularly Vindaloo and Phall curries, and if in the next few days you still have excess flatulence, then see your GP,' I advised.

'What, so there's nothing…' he paused for a moment. Then came a loud *PAAAAARP!* '…you can do for it?' he said, finishing his question.

'Not right now, no. But don't worry, the gas will pass, pardon the pun,' I said.

'Then what's the bloody point of this out-of-hours service?' he queried.

'Well, it's for health concerns that cannot wait until the in-hours GP surgeries are open,' I politely informed him.

'I can't wait until Monday though, Doctor!' he said, in an irate tone.

'Rest assured, Joe, curry induced flatulence is not an urgent or life-threatening condition that requires the immediate attention from a doctor. Flatulence can be a common side effect of hot and spicy food, and it's nature's way of dispersing gas from the gastrointestinal tract,' I said to reassure him. To which he rudely replied with,

'Nature's way my arse!' and immediately hung up on me! Charming. It's a shame he hung up on me as I was about to offer him some further advice. I would've advised him that whenever he indulges in a hot curry, then to place a toilet roll in the fridge for the following morning. I'm only joking; I wouldn't have said that on a recorded line. It's a good tip, though!

Caught Short

It was 4pm on a very hot summer, Friday afternoon. My ambulance technician crewmate, Jamie, and I were sat in the station mess room relaxing after barely stopping since the start of our twelve hour shift. A short time later, we were passed, via the station telephone, details of a GP urgent admission into the surgical ward of the infirmary. An 'urgent admission' meant that blue lights and sirens were not required; we were permitted – well, legally obliged – to simply trundle along to the given address under normal driving conditions. The doctor had visited the elderly man, our patient, at his home earlier that afternoon and diagnosed him with 'Faecal Impaction', and so she had arranged an ambulance to convey him direct to the ward, therefore bypassing the A&E department.

For those who don't know what Faecal Impaction is, it's a huge lump of dehydrated, firm stool that becomes lodged in the bowels or close to the rectum. It is most often seen – though perhaps *seen* is not the ideal choice of word in the circumstances – in people who are constipated for a long period of time. You wish you hadn't asked now, don't you.

So Jamie and I made our way to the address given. On our arrival, we vacated the cab and proceeded toward the front door. There we were met by the patient's wife, who kindly escorted us to the lounge where her husband, Jack, was sat in an armchair. The first thing I noticed was that he was clutching his stomach, evidently in a lot of pain and discomfort. The second thing I noticed was that he was wearing a dog collar. No, not the studded type usually seen on British Bulldogs; I mean the type that men and women of 'the cloth' wear.

I introduced both Jamie and I to Jack, a clergyman – I can't remember what 'rank' he was, so I'll keep it simple. As I was questioning him, his elderly wife passed me a hand written letter that the visiting GP had left for me to read and then give to the receiving surgical ward doctor. Reading the letter, it became apparent that Jack hadn't opened his bowels for eleven days and, to no surprise, was experiencing abdominal pain as a consequence. Having established that Jack was in too much pain to walk to the ambulance, we decided to assist him, by wheeling him out of the lounge on the carry-chair and into the hot, humid saloon of the ambulance, asking him to sit upright on the stretcher. Upon him doing as I asked, I then advised him to bend his legs and draw his knees up toward his stomach, as that provides a great form of positional analgesia when suffering from abdominal pain.

After undertaking a set of baseline observations on him – that is, respiratory rate, heart rate, blood pressure, temperature, blood glucose and a standard ECG – I questioned him about his perceived pain score. He scored it as an eight out of ten. He was evidently in a lot of pain, so I asked him if he would like me to give him some pain relief in the form of morphine. He consented to the pain relief, but informed me that phlebotomists – NHS staff that obtain blood samples from a patient – usually struggle to find a vein. Nevertheless, he was in agony, so I was willing to give him the benefit of the doubt and try at least twice. So that is what I did... and I missed both times. That taught me to never underestimate the skills of a phlebotomist!

With no IV access obtained and Jack writhing around in agony on the stretcher, I felt helpless. Entonox, a.k.a. 'gas and air', wasn't a suitable option, as it can sometimes worsen abdominal pain and, therefore, had the potential to increase Jack's perceived pain score above his already stated eight out of ten. So, after securing Jack on the stretcher with safety belts, we were ready to convey him to hospital.

Glancing at my wristwatch, I noted that it was now 5pm... on a Friday! The traffic was going to be congested and we anticipated a long, drawn-out journey to the hospital, which was nine miles from the address. For that reason, I asked Jamie to use blue lights and sirens for the journey. I informed Jack that, due to me not being able to give him any pain relief, we were going to get him through the rush hour traffic and into hospital as quickly as possible, explaining that doctors are usually more competent at obtaining IV access than paramedics – the doctor would attempt cannulation and administer some morphine to him. Jack acknowledged my plan but continued to display signs of severe pain and discomfort on the stretcher.

Leaving me to complete my paperwork in the saloon of the vehicle, Jamie adopted his position in the driving seat and we headed off to hospital under emergency driving conditions as planned. However, leaving the housing estate was a bit of a bumpy ride, as there were numerous 'sleeping policemen' – you'd think they'd have something better to do, wouldn't you? Jamie hit the first four of them at 20MPH, causing Jack's backside to lift off the stretcher mattress a few inches.

'Oooh! Arrrgh!' he cried out after each of them, prompting me to tell Jamie to take the remaining speed humps slowly.

After several minutes, we approached the accelerating lane of the dual carriageway, eager to make full use of its national speed limit, 70MPH. Jamie slipped the gears into third, accelerated up the gradient and joined the carriageway. The engine revved noisily. He accelerated some more, slipped into fourth gear, by now reaching a speed of 50MPH plus, then moved to the outside lane, overtaking numerous vehicles, before slipping into fifth and accelerating to 60, 70, 80MPH.

We sustained 80MPH for a good three miles, albeit having to occasionally weave from the outside lane to the inside lane and vice-versa, to avoid inattentive motorists that hadn't noticed an ambulance swiftly approaching from behind. I frequently glanced up at Jack to see how he was. No improvement. Not that any was expected, to be fair.

As we continued to hurtle along the carriageway, Jamie shouted from the cab.

'Andy, roundabout coming up, mate!' That meant that the ambulance would be swinging around to the right. I could feel the vehicle slow down as Jamie eased off the accelerator on approaching the roundabout. He applied pressure to the brakes, slipped into third gear and fed the steering wheel through his hands, using the pull-push technique to manoeuvre the ambulance around the roundabout. Quickly shifting his steering wheel hard left, he then accelerated and took the third exit. He snapped the gearstick back into fourth, applying more weight to the gas pedal before slipping into fifth gear and once again hurtling passed an abundance of Friday rush hour traffic.

Several more minutes of driving at breakneck speed passed by, including more weaving in and out of lanes, busy junctions and first, second and third exits of roundabouts. Jack continued to writhe around in pain on the stretcher. He looked white, as if he'd been rolled in a sack of flour, so I stood and popped my head through the window that separates the cab from the saloon and said to Jamie,

'Slow down a bit, mate, you're giving Jack a white-knuckle ride.'

'OK mate. We're gonna hit a tailback now anyway,' he said, as we approached the notoriously congested town traffic. I sat back down in my seat and cast my eyes over Jack; he was by now not only grey, but severely grimacing, too.

'Are you OK, Jack? We're nearly there; we've just got to get through town now.'

'I don't think I'm gonna make it,' he said, with a look of impending doom on his face.

'What do you mean, you don't think you're gonna make it?' I asked, fearing he thought he was going to die.

'I need to open my bowels!' he informed me.

'You've needed to open your bowels for damn near two weeks,' I thought, 'why all of a sudden now, in the back of the bloody ambulance… with me here?!' But I said nothing. Instead, I stood and glanced out of a window to see what our location was… we were approximately five minutes away from the hospital. Trouble was, the designated ward was another five minutes' walk from the ambulance parking bay.

'Jack, can you hold on for another ten minutes or so?' I asked.

'I'll try,' he said, clutching his backside with his right hand.

By now we'd hit full-on congested, Friday rush hour traffic. With blue lights flashing and sirens wailing, Jamie proceeded by straddling the centre between left and right side lanes of a built-up area of town, occasionally weaving in and out of traffic. Countless motorists heading in the same direction in front of us parted to the left, mounting the kerb, while oncoming traffic parted to their left. It was absolute chaos! After a few more minutes, I stood to peer through the windscreen to view our exact location, then turned to Jack and said,

'Five minutes, Jack, five minutes.'

'I'm not gonna be able to hold it, it's coming,' he said, providing me with too much information.

'Never mind man of the cloth,' I thought, 'he's probably touching cloth!' But instead I replied with, 'Do your best, Jack; we're nearly there!' attempting to encourage and reassure him.

'I can't! I can't!' he said while laid on his left side, facing away from me, clutching his butt cheeks with his right hand.

'Do your best, Jack; we're nearly there!' I said, repeating my encouragement. But, moments later, to my horror, Jack shouted,

'It's coming! It's coming!'

For a split second, time stood still. 'Blimey', I thought, 'the last time I heard a patient say that in the back of an ambulance, I delivered a baby!' Then, to my dismay, a mahoosive lump swiftly accumulated in the backside of Jack's trousers, revealing a large wet patch. Almost instantaneously came the shock of the stench and the imaginary green mist alerting my olfactory sense; the most unimaginable aroma of eleven days' worth of shit filled the saloon of the ambulance.

I couldn't help but repetitively retch, and my eyes began streaming. As the bulge in the arse end of his trousers grew bigger, Jack's face displayed the Oxford English Dictionary's definition

119

of relief; that is to say: *A feeling of reassurance and relaxation following release from anxiety or distress!*

As the noxious fumes became progressively worse, I had no choice but to once again pop my head through the small window that separates the cab and the saloon, but this time for some much needed air. While inhaling fresh air from the breezy cab, I whispered to Jamie,

'You've cured him, mate.'

'You what?' he asked, taking his eyes off the road momentarily to look at me.

'You've cured him. Your white-knuckle driving has caused Jack to shit himself, literally shit himself! He's just soiled his trousers with eleven days' worth of shit!'

On that comment, Jamie burst out laughing, and then immediately did what any ambulance man or woman with a dark, sick and twisted sense of humour would do to their crewmate – and friend – in those circumstances on a very hot summer's day... He switched the saloon heating on, causing the already intolerable pong to become even more unbearable!

When we arrived at the hospital, I placed a blanket over Jack for dignity purposes, so nobody could see the huge protruding bulge and the moist patch spread across the arse end of his trousers. Though, there was no getting away from the smell, which was overpowering to say the least; to say the very least!

Jamie lowered the ramp and we wheeled the stretcher from the saloon, through the entrance of the hospital and along the corridors to the surgical ward. Upon arrival, I explained to the receiving ward sister, out of earshot of anybody else, that Jack had been admitted with faecal impaction, but had opened his bowels en route to the hospital. The sister then casually strolled over to Jack, who still lay on the stretcher, with the intention of politely introducing herself to him. But instead of welcoming and informing him of which bed space he had been allocated, she had to quickly take several steps back as a consequence of the overpowering whiff being emitted from Jack's arse!

A Drunken Frivolity

My colleague, Kevin, a fellow paramedic, was parked up in an ambulance bay at the A&E department late one evening, having recently admitted a patient. On vacating the ward and approaching his ambulance, he was alarmed, and unamused, to find a man sat in the passenger seat of the cab. Standing on the passenger side, Kevin abruptly opened the door and said,

'Get out of the ambulance, now!'

'Giza-lift home, mate,' was the man's response to Kevin's firm instruction, albeit with slow, slurred words.

'No, I won't give you a lift home! This is an ambulance not a bloody taxi, now get out!' Kevin replied, once again with assertion.

'Go on pal, giza-lift,' he asked once again, barely comprehensible.

'I've told you no, now get out of the cab!' he instructed for the third time.

The man wouldn't budge though, and Kevin obviously didn't want to drag him out of the ambulance, as that would constitute assault and battery. So, initially clueless as to what to do, he was stuck between a rock and a hard place. However, a minute or so later, after further attempts at instructing the man to get out of the ambulance, Kevin spotted a police officer sat in his marked car near the entrance to the hospital. So he trundled over to the officer, and as he got closer to the car, the officer wound down his window.

'Hiya mate, everything okay?' the police officer asked.

'No, not really mate. Can you come and get this clown out the cab of my ambulance, please?' Kevin politely asked. 'He's inebriated and asking for a lift home. I've told him, no, but he won't budge.'

The police officer stepped out of his patrol car, and with Kevin alongside him, they began walking back over to the ambulance. As they got nearer to the drunken man sat in what *he* perceived to be a

123

'Free, Big Yellow Taxi', the officer, with a look of surprise on his face, turned to Kevin and said,

'Blimey mate, you weren't kidding, were you?' The officer was shocked to find that the drunken man was literally dressed as a clown! The cheeky little scrote had been out all afternoon and evening revelling at a fancy dress party. On the police officer's instruction, he did, of course, swiftly get out of the cab, and staggered on home... or maybe to the circus!

TWOC

My good friend, now retired ambulance technician, Bill, was inside a house assessing his patient, alongside his crewmate, Dave, a paramedic, on an estate similar to that of an earlier story; an estate of the kind commonly known to ambulance personnel as Scrotesville. In case you've forgotten, Scrotesville is a communal area where an abundance of scrotes reside, and a scrote is a male with low character, who is idle, thoughtless, inconsiderate, and disrespectful, with bad manners, no moral fibre and often with a poor appearance.

Bill and Dave had their middle-aged male patient secured on their carry-chair and were ready to vacate the premises. As they lifted the carry-chair over the threshold of the front door, it became apparent, on observing the roadside where the ambulance had been parked, that it was no longer there. Scratching his head, Bill said,

'Where the bloody hell—?'

'Where 'ave you parked?' the patient asked, interrupting Bill. 'You could've parked outside my house, there's plenty of room!' he emphasised.

'I did!' Dave said.

For a moment, Dave began to think he may have forgotten to apply the handbrake and the vehicle had rolled down the hill as a result. But there was no obvious sign of carnage at the bottom of the hill.

'I parked it there, outside the house,' Dave said, pointing to the roadside. 'Where the bloody hell is it?!'

Shocked at the mysterious disappearance, Bill left Dave with the patient sat on the carry-chair and went to explore the whereabouts of the ambulance. After a minute or so, and only a moment away from contacting ambulance control to report the vehicle as missing, presumed stolen, the ambulance appeared in the distance and Bill watched as it was driven back to the spot where it had been originally parked. Driving the ambulance was the textbook definition of a scrote, an eighteen year old one, approximately.

Now, Bill was an old school ambulance man and not the most tolerant of people, and absolutely despised youthful scrotes. The scrote applied the handbrake, put the gears into neutral, switched the engine off – leaving the keys in the ignition – and vacated the cab with a huge grin on his face, then walked around the opposite side of the ambulance toward his house.

Disgruntled Bill stomps over and grabs him by the scruff of his filthy sweater with one hand, and by his throat with the other, and begins questioning him.

'What the f**k do you think you're doing, taking my ambulance for a drive, you f**kin' cheeky little f**kin' scrote?!' Bill asked, while holding the thief's head firmly against the side of the ambulance. 'Do you realise, by law, that's classed as taking without the owner's consent?!'

'It's an ambulance, you're not the f**kin' owner!' was the scrote's dumb-ass reply, though barely comprehensible due to having his face held forcefully against the side of the ambulance. The scrote's bold reply made the already extremely displeased Bill even more intolerant, and so he demonstrated his fury by not only giving him a verbal dressing down, but by banging the thief's head against the side of the ambulance as he did so.

'Don't...' *Bang!* '...you ever f**kin'...' *Bang!* '...take a f**kin' ambulance again...' *Bang!* '...you *f***kin' thieving...' *Bang!* '...little scrote!' Bill said, with his teeth clenched together aggressively.

Dave and the patient, situated just fifteen metres or so away, looked on in horror as the unorthodox justice was handed out to the thief. Bill then let go of the young man, who swiftly ran away toward his house, obviously dazed.

They were the days when you could get away with such behaviour. Today? No chance!

Twister

It was 3pm on Christmas day, and my crewmate, Ben, an ambulance technician, and I had barely stopped since the commencement of our twelve hour shift. In addition to several 'bread and butter' type incidents, we'd earlier attended to an elderly lady, on a 'turkey and tinsel' holiday, who was in cardiac arrest. On our arrival inside the hotel restaurant, we found her seated, but keeled over with her face in her Christmas dinner at the dining table.

What made that sad incident a little humorous for Ben and I wasn't the unfortunate position we found her in, but how the other thirty or so residents, dining around her, didn't bat an eyelid; they just carried on eating their dinners while we attempted to resuscitate her in the restaurant, unfortunately without success. Some periodically glimpsed at the deceased elderly lady and, without any facial expression of compassion whatsoever, continued chewing on their turkey. Incredible!

Anyway, we were sat in the station mess room enjoying a well-earned cuppa when, after just several slurps, my hand portable radio alarmed.

'Go ahead, over,' I said.

'Roger, emergency call to a forty-four year old female with back pain, over,' the dispatcher said.

'Roger, understood,' I replied. So Ben and I vacated the station and adopted our positions in the ambulance – him driving and me in the attendant's seat. Ben activated the blue lights and sirens and within several minutes we arrived, grabbed the appropriate equipment, including the Entonox, from the saloon of the vehicle and strode purposefully toward the front door already ajar anticipating our arrival.

On stepping inside the property, we were met by a man who was a little tipsy. He escorted us to the lounge, where we were pleasantly welcomed by a room full of adults, teens and young children; they were obviously having a typical festive, family get-together. Directly in front of us, laid on the carpeted lounge room floor, were three adults collapsed in a heap, face down on top of each other on the colourful, large, spotted mat of the globally notorious game called 'Twister'. The lady at the bottom of the pile, Janet, our patient, could clearly be heard groaning.

Ben and I knelt down on the floor, and I began ascertaining a lowdown of events from another of the family members present.

'OK, what's been going on here then?' I asked. A lady, who was also a little tipsy, then began to give details.

'Well, as you can see, those three were playing Twister. They were all tangled up, so to speak, and on the last two instructions of 'left hand on blue' and 'right foot on yellow', they collapsed in a heap, and Janet said her lower back had gone into spasm,' she explained and in a comprehensible manner, surprisingly.

'I see. Why haven't the two blokes got up, though; their weight on top of her isn't going to help her back pain, is it?' I asked with curiosity. Frank, another adult present – identified by his named Christmas party hat – then spoke.

'I know, but Janet screamed at them not to move. They were going to move but it caused her unbearable pain. She said she'd kill them if they moved before the paramedics arrived,' Frank said, chuckling to himself, evidently merry from the effects of copious amounts of alcohol.

As this discussion was happening, Janet was, obviously, almost motionless due to the spasm in her back, and from the fear of experiencing excruciating pain if she moved in the slightest.

'OK. Does she have any existing back problems at all, such as slipped discs or anything else?' I asked.

'No, she's never had any significant back complaint until today,' Frank explained.

We'd been on scene just a couple of minutes, and while questioning, I was weighing up the logistics of how best to get the two men off of Janet's back, so that we could get *her* off the floor. I crouched down a little lower and made eye contact with Janet, who was grimacing and groaning. Every slight, voluntary move she made, to attempt some position of comfort, caused her to wince and cry out in pain.

'Hello Janet, my name's Andy, I'm going to help you. Now, I think it would be best if we start you on gas 'n' air. That may be just enough relief for your lower back pain to get the two blokes off you, OK?' I said, as Ben prepared the Entonox.

'Yeah, OK,' she replied, before giving out a scream, as merely raising her head off the floor to answer me caused her severe pain. I handed her the Entonox tubing with mouthpiece attached, and instructed her how to use it correctly. Janet began inhaling deep, and the sound of compressed gas leaving the cylinder with each inhalation resonated around the room. I looked at the position of the three of them, and the position Janet's arms were in amongst the tangled heap of bodies. It became clear to me that I'd need the two blokes off her in order to obtain IV access in one of her arms and provide a more potent drug i.e., morphine sulphate.

In the background, I could hear various family members, evidently under heavy influence of alcohol, discussing the coloured spot of the Twister mat they'd have gone for had they been playing. While I was pondering over the best plan of action, I could hear, albeit in slurred speech,

'Well, when Janet was bent over, if she'd put her left hand on that blue spot that's second one down, and put her right foot on that yellow spot that's second one down, then she probably wouldn't 'ave collapsed anyway!' the voice emphasised with game-playing confidence. Then a different voice was heard, once again slurred.

'You say that, but he got his left hand on that blue spot that's second one down before Janet even moved. The rules state that players aren't allowed to use the same spot, so she couldn't 'ave gone for that blue spot,' he said, prompting me to turn my head and enquire with interest,

'Are you not?'

'No, mate,' he replied, while stood holding a can of lager in his hand and rocking back and forth, his eyes not fully focussing. 'It says it in the rules. It says that each player must try to place the called-out body part on a vacant circle of the called-out colour. That means there can never be more than one hand or foot on any one circle,' he said, educating me.

'Well, I never knew that,' I replied with intrigue. Moments later, Janet, releasing her lips from the mouthpiece of the gas and air, shouted,

'Who gives a f**kin' toss what the rules are, I'm in agony here! Can we just get on with relieving my pain and gettin' me off this f**kin' mat!'

'Oops,' I thought, 'something's rattled her cage!' So once again, I glanced at the intricate positions the three of them were in, and lowered my body position to make eye contact with Janet for a second time. 'Is that gas 'n' air helping, Janet? Do you think we could try and get them two off you now?'

'No, no! Please don't move them! I need stronger pain relief... arrrgh! ...before they move,' she said, eventually finishing her sentence. Then one of the other collapsed players yelled,

'Well, I'm bloody uncomfortable too, Janet, not just you!' Their shouting prompted several of the other adults to ask them to calm down, as it was becoming a little heated.

By now it had occurred to me that this wasn't going to be as straightforward as I first thought; I was going to have to give the two blokes on top some precise instructions so I'd be able to have a clear view of one of Janet's arms and reach it to obtain IV access. After asking the other two players their names, I began to plan in advance each strategic manoeuvre, hoping that asking them to reposition their limbs would prove helpful to the predicament we were all in.

As Ben prepared the morphine – prematurely as far as I was concerned – I rummaged in the paramedic bag and removed the

132

appropriate packaged items I'd need, ready for if, or when, I'd repositioned both Keith and Terry in a way that provided clear access to cannulate.

'OK, here we go. Keith, I need you to put your left hand on yellow,' I said, grinning to myself at the thought of a paramedic acting the part of 'caller' while playing Twister on duty on Christmas day. This may all seem too bizarre to be true, but believe me, it is! Following my instruction, Keith carefully moved his left hand as I'd asked.

'Now, Terry, I need you to put your right hand on that red, there...' I said, placing the tip of my index finger on the designated spot. '...and preferably your left foot on that third blue down from your head end.' Terry carefully repositioned his right hand and his left foot. In doing so, Janet screamed out in pain once more, but now that Terry and Keith were repositioned, I peered through the gap between the tangled players to see if I'd be able to cannulate. On close inspection, there was still no chance!

'No, it's no good,' I said. 'I still can't get to either of her arms. We're gonna have to try repositioning again.' That prompted a barrage of expletives to be hurled around the room from the frustrated Janet, who was feeling very little relief from the gas and air.

'OK, this time, Terry, move your left hand to that fourth blue down,' I instructed, 'and your right foot to that last red. Keith, I want you to put your left foot on that third blue down.' Hoping that would prove helpful to my objective, I watched with the anticipation of an obsessively keen player as Keith and Terry carefully manoeuvred their limbs. But as they came to rest on the requested coloured spots, it became apparent that both had their left foot on the same blue. On noticing this, a drunken 'Mr Twister rules expert' piped up with,

'They've got their feet on the same blue spot; they'd be disqualified if this was a proper game.'

His comment set off not only a further barrage of obscenities from

133

Janet, but also from Keith and Terry, who were by now dripping with sweat from the sheer intensity of holding themselves in awkward positions.

While several onlooking family members calmed the heated atmosphere once again, I peered through the tangled players, adjusting my angle slightly until I was relieved to see a gap through to Janet's arm. Satisfied I'd be able to cannulate, I went about cutting one of the sleeves of Janet's Christmas sweater, and it wasn't long before I'd obtained IV access. I then administered the euphoric morphine to her, to such relief that Keith and Terry were able to remove themselves from the mat... both vowing never to play Twister ever again, as too did Janet!

Mr Gadget

I'm no *Star Trek* fan but I found this next anecdote very amusing when it was recited to me in the station mess room.

In the fictional *Star Trek* universe, there is a multifunctional hand-held device used for sensor scanning, data analysis and data recording. The name for the device is a tricorder. An electronic replica of the device could be purchased by anybody and so, as a *Star Trek* fan, Jed, a veteran paramedic and former colleague of mine, was enthralled when he received a tricorder replica as a gift.

One lovely summer's day, Jed and his crewmate, Mitch, were dispatched to the High Street, as a Good Samaritan had rung treble-nine and stated that a man was laid unconscious alongside a public bench. On arrival at the scene they immediately recognised that the patient was Buster, so they took the appropriate equipment from the saloon of the ambulance and walked briskly over to him. There they listened to the Good Samaritan's history of events leading up to her ringing for an ambulance.

Jed informed her that they knew Buster, and explained to her that he was a local homeless man and a regular patient of theirs. Happy that she'd done her bit, Jed thanked her for calling and she continued along the High Street and went about her business.

Mitch and Jed crouched down alongside Buster, and Jed shouted his name while shaking his shoulders. Buster consequently roused, opened his eyes and began slurring some incomprehensible words. Looking around the bench, Jed and Mitch took note of the abundance of empty cans of Diamond White Cider, a seven point five percent alcohol by volume (ABV) strength beverage, strewn across the ground. After a few minutes of encouraging Buster to sit up against the bench and cooperate with them, he did so. Jed then began questioning him on whether he was experiencing any symptoms.

'Buster, how are you feeling at the moment?' Jed asked.

'Dizzy,' he slurred.

'Anything else?'

'Back ache!' he stated, grimacing.

'Well you have been lying on the concrete pavement, haven't you, Buster?!' Jed emphasised.

'Yeah, but why am I dizzy and why 'ave I got back ache and 'eadache and can't see straight and everything?' Buster enquired with concern. 'Is it pancreatitis? I've had that before.'

'Do you have any pain in your stomach or anywhere else other than your head and back?' Jed asked, with relevance as the condition Buster stated usually presents with severe abdominal pain.

'No, but I think my back pain might be summot serious,' Buster mumbled.

'Mmm,' Jed hummed with scepticism, before he said, 'Mitch, we're gonna have to scan him, mate!'

'Scan me? What do you mean?' asked Buster, once again his speech slurred. At the same time, Mitch looked at Jed as if to say *'Scan him? What do you mean?'*.

'Go-go Gadget Tricorder,' Jed said, revealing his much loved toy from the large pocket of his trouser leg. Confused at the device, which he'd no idea Jed had in his possession, Mitch frowned at him but said nothing, as he suspected Jed was up to something funny.

'What's that?' mumbled Buster, while pointing shakily at the device.

'Well,' said Jed, holding the tricorder in front of Buster's face, 'this is a new piece of ambulance equipment; when we can't come to a diagnosis, we basically scan down the front of the patient's body and it'll tell us what's wrong with them.'

'Blimey, today's technology, hey!' Buster said, with garbled speech and an alcohol induced gaze that meant his left eye was looking *at* Jed and his right eye was looking *for* Jed!

136

'I know, it's brilliant isn't it!' Jed said, looking admiringly at the tricorder as if it really was some instant medical diagnostic tool. 'It tells us everything we need to know. It's foolproof!'

So Jed, with the device in his hand, scanned down the front of Buster, who was sat upright against the park bench, slowly waving it from head to toe and then in a reverse motion. Mitch stood with his hand held over his mouth, hiding his grin, while Buster attempted to follow the device going up and down his body, but had difficulty staying focussed on it. Jed then stared at the device, nodding his head as if reassured at the diagnosis.

'Do you know what's wrong with me?' Buster asked.

'Mmm, I do, yeah,' Jed replied with certainty in his voice.

'What does it say's wrong with me?' Buster asked with concern. Jed gazed at Buster with a very solemn facial expression and said,

'It says you're pissed!'

Mirror, Mirror on the Wall…

While driving back to the ambulance station, having recently cleared from the A&E department, my paramedic crewmate, Philip, and I were passed the address of a sixty-five year old gent who was experiencing chest pain. On blue lights and sirens, we proceeded in the direction of the given address, vacating the cab and grabbing the appropriate equipment on our arrival, then hurried down the garden pathway. I opened the unlocked front door. We both stepped over the threshold and I shouted,

'Hello, ambulance service!'

'Up here! In the bedroom,' a male voice summoned us from upstairs. So Philip and I ascended the staircase and entered the bedroom where our patient, Arthur, was sat on his bed with his back to us but facing a mirror. Before we even introduced ourselves, Philip and I just looked at each other, silently acknowledging the never-before-seen choice of facial hair design of the man's reflection in the mirror. With both of us placing a hand over our mouths to discreetly hide the beaming grin on our faces, I couldn't help but imagine Arthur staring in the mirror and singing to himself *'Mirror, mirror on the wall, whose facial hair design looks the silliest of all?'*.

Trying to keep a straight face – which was mightily difficult, as I could see with my peripheral vision Philip smirking beside me – I began by asking Arthur some questions related to the chest pain he was experiencing.

'Arthur, what time did your chest pain start?' I asked.

'About nine o'clock,' he slurred, intermittently clutching and rubbing his chest with his right hand.

'And what were you doing when the pain came on?'

'Well, I was doing my ablutions in the bathroom, and I started feelin' sleepy, and then this awful pain came across my chest,' he explained, intermittently slurring.

'Were you brushing your teeth vigorously, or something, when the pain came on?' I asked with relevance, as that could constitute exertion.

'No, no, no, no,' he repeated as if intoxicated. 'I didn't get as far as brushin' me teeth,' he said, in garbled speech.

'Arthur, I notice you're slurring your words a little, have you been drinking at all?' I asked as a rhetorical question, as I knew he had; I could smell it on his breath!

'Yeah, yeah, yeah,' he repeated, nodding his head. 'I've 'ad a few cheeky, cheeky whiskeys, yeah,' he answered.

'Only a few?' I thought, but instead said, 'Ok, no problem. Arthur, I need to ask you some more questions about your chest pain, and we need to carry out a number of tests on you, and administer some drugs etcetera, obviously with your consent. Then we'll have to take you through to the A 'n' E, to see the doc,' I explained.

To keep a long story short – since the procedures undertaken for chest pain are quite complex – I'll just tell you that Arthur consented to a visit to the hospital for further assessment. So while I undertook pertinent tests, and additional questioning, Philip went to fetch the carry-chair from the ambulance. Within twenty minutes or so, we'd carried out all necessary interventions in the ambulance and were ready to convey Arthur to hospital. Throughout the journey, I couldn't help but periodically raise a smile every time I glanced at Arthur's unusual appearance.

On arriving inside the A&E department, we wheeled our patient, sat semi-recumbent on the stretcher, along the corridor toward the receiving triage sister. She glanced down at Arthur, who was by now zonked out, chuckled to herself, and asked,

'What have you brought him in for, to finish off his personal grooming?' I giggled at her witty comment, and then said,

'No, chest pain, actually, but I'm not convinced it's cardiac in nature.'

'OK. Why is he fast asleep, has he been drinking?' she asked.

'Yeah, he's half-cut!' I replied. The sister immediately laughed, glancing back down at Arthur, who had a beard on the left side of his face, but the right hand side was as smooth as a baby's bum!

We later found out the reason why. It turned out that while Arthur was under the influence of half a bottle of whiskey, he'd stupidly decided to give himself a cut-throat shave! Hardly the wisest or safest time to partake in a spot of personal grooming of that kind. Fortunately, his skill with a cut-throat razor left him unmarked. Unfortunately, the chest pain experienced mid shave left his face and facial hair asymmetrical!

After being diagnosed with heartburn – probably caused by drinking copious amounts of whiskey that morning – he was discharged home several hours later where, I assume, he finished off his cut-throat shave, leaving his de-bearded face looking symmetrical again!

Pun Intended!

In the medical profession there are three forms of analgesia used by health care professionals. They are: positional, pharmacological, and distractional. An example of positional is, as mentioned in an earlier story, drawing the knees toward the chest to reduce abdominal pain. Pharmacological analgesia involves the use of over-the-counter medicines, such as Paracetamol, or prescription-only and controlled medicines, such as codeine and IV morphine. Distractional analgesia, as the name suggests, involves the health care professional in distracting the suffering patient in one of a number of ways, though this form *usually* only works on young children. For example, inflating a protective nitrile glove so that the five fingers resemble the comb and points found on the top of a chicken's head. Once the glove is inflated and tied off, a face is drawn on the ballooned body of the glove, which is then handed to the child, who in *most* cases finds it very funny, therefore taking their mind off the pain. Brilliant!

As I said, distractional analgesia works best on young children. However, there have been a fair number of incidences where my crewmate and I successfully used distractional analgesia to reduce the pain of an adult patient. One particular incident springs to mind that not only had the patient in stitches, but her husband and two teenaged children, too! Allow me to explain.

My ambulance technician crewmate, Thomas, and I were dispatched to a forty year old female who had slipped on her recently mopped, wet kitchen floor, and had landed very awkwardly, subsequently sustaining a lower left leg injury. On our arrival inside the patient's kitchen, with appropriate equipment to hand, we were presented with a lady, Karen, lying on her back, screaming in absolute agony. Also in the kitchen was her husband, understandably concerned for his wife, and their two teenaged children – a girl and a boy – who also appeared very upset and worried. On examination of Karen's left leg, it was obvious that she'd sustained a closed fracture, as it was clearly deformed.

Thomas and I crouched down beside Karen and began by introducing ourselves. I then commenced some pertinent questioning regarding her symptoms, past medical history, allergies and so on, while Thomas began undertaking some appropriate clinical observations. As we carried out our self-designated tasks, I offered Karen 'gas and air', as an interim analgesic; however, she refused it as she'd had it on a previous occasion and had experienced severe vomiting as a consequence. So, I asked her if she would consent to me obtaining IV access, and administering some Metoclopramide – an anti-sickness/nausea drug – and the potent analgesic, morphine sulphate. After gaining her consent, I applied a tourniquet to her left arm and began to palpate for a suitable vein. As I was doing that, I attempted to distract her a little by asking her some open ended questions.

'So, Karen, do you work at all?' I asked, tapping on an area of her left arm where a good, accessible vein can usually be found.

'Arrrgh! Yeah. I'm a dentist,' she informed me as she screamed out, displaying a mouth full of beautifully aligned, pearly white teeth. Her profession immediately gave me an idea to try to distract her from the pain while I continued searching for a vein, and so initiated a series of profession-based wisecracks – granted not my own original puns, but nevertheless, apt. So responding to Karen's answer, I said,

'A dentist! Wow, that must be a *full-filling* job; better than having the same old *grind* day after day, hey?' Thomas immediately followed with a vocal '*boom boom cchhh!*', the musical sound usually played on percussion instruments to punctuate jokes, more uncommonly known as 'the sting'. Karen immediately stopped grimacing and instead laughed out loud, as too did her husband and children.

As they all chuckled, I continued questioning Karen while palpating her left arm for a viable vein.

'Which dentist do you work at, Karen?' I asked.

'Old Oak Road,' she answered, still smiling broadly from my

previous wholly intended pun.

'Oh, right. Is that a permanent job or are you just *filling in*?' Thomas immediately followed with another vocal '*boom boom cchhh!*', and Karen, her husband and the two children elevated their screams of amusement. As the laughing continued, Karen replied,

'It's permanent,' then followed shortly after with a barrage of expletives provoked by the sheer pain in her leg. Thomas, recognising that humorous puns had distracted Karen from the pain, albeit momentarily, swiftly followed her answer with,

'Did you get that job by word of mouth?' On that the room instantaneously filled with more laughter. It was lovely to see the kids go from appearing upset to looking so relaxed and thoroughly enjoying themselves, despite their mother's quite serious injury.

After a short period of palpating, I'd located a suitable vein to cannulate, and so rummaged through the paramedic bag for the appropriate consumables. However, as the distractional puns had momentarily ceased, Karen began concentrating on the pain again and subsequently cried out.

'Arrrgh, shit! My bloody leg is killin'!' she exclaimed. With distraction still my only analgesic option, I had to think quickly, and so with a tone of authority in my voice, as if talking to my own child, I shouted,

'Hey, less of that language or I'll rinse your mouth out!' Thomas swiftly responded to my pun with,

'Don't shout at her Andy, or her husband will *crown* you!'

The fitting comments provided some more temporary distraction for Karen, and prompted her family to burst into laughter for the fourth time. The apt, spontaneous wit was having some positive effect, including reassurance to Karen's family, as they appeared increasingly calmer and less concerned about the severity of Karen's injury. As the laughter around the kitchen settled, Thomas asked,

'Remind me, who's the boss of that dental surgery, isn't it Phil McCavity?' It may have been an old one but his pun triggered yet more laughter around the room, and Karen's yelling and grimacing lessened as she belly laughed while laid on her back on the floor. It was short-lived analgesia but it was working, as she appeared a lot more composed during those brief spells, occasionally giggling as our words reverberated in her head.

With a vein engorged, I donned a pair of nitrile gloves, cleaned the skin around the desired access site, and removed a cannula from its packaging. I held Karen's right arm with my left hand, and with the cannula ready in my right hand I then said,

'Ok, here we go. *Brace* yourself, Karen.' Despite the circumstances, her reaction was spontaneous as she let out a delightful laugh. Her husband and children were keeled over, clutching their stomachs. As the fun continued, I hovered the cannula over my chosen venous access site, and then said,

'I'll try not to hurt you, Karen; I don't want to upset you, I know you've got fillings too.' Yet more hilarity echoed round the room, and tears of laughter were by now rolling down Karen's face! So while she was distracted, I pierced the skin of her arm with the needle, entered the vein, and obtained and secured patent IV access. Thomas handed me the now prepared anti-sickness drug, which I administered first. Then he handed me the morphine sulphate. Prior to pushing any morphine through the open port of the cannula, I said to Karen,

'If, after I've administered a small dose of morphine, you experience any side effects that you can't tolerate—'

'You don't need to explain to her, mate,' Thomas said, interrupting me. 'She's a dentist, so she knows the drill!'

Everyone immediately burst into laughter for the umpteenth time, and tears rolled down the children's cheeks. As the chuckling continued and the family members used their palms to wipe their tears, I administered some morphine to Karen, then gradually watched her pain visibly reduce considerably over several minutes, to the point where no more dental puns were necessary to distract her. Job done!

Throughout my career in the ambulance service, a variety of crewmates and I used patients' professions, such as electricians, plumbers, and painters and decorators, to name but a few, as the topic for apt, humorous puns to provide distractional analgesia. In fact, to such incredible success that I think it is certainly safe to say that laughter really is the best medicine!

Epilogue

Well, there you have it, an insight into the *Lighter Side* of working on *the Dark Side*. There are plenty more humorous stories I could share with you, of course, and in great detail, but I daren't! They're far too outrageous, distasteful and wholly unsuitable for publication and exposure to the general public – those stories will probably forever be confined to the mess room! Internal consumption only!

Others... well, I only have brief memories of. For example, the man who rang treble-nine and stated that he'd cut his throat while shaving, and was bleeding to death. On the crew's arrival, they found what first appeared to be blood all over the place, from the bathroom to the lounge, all over the television screen, glass cabinets and other furniture. The crew, however, smelt a rat... well, not a rat, diluted Ketchup to be precise. What the man's reasons behind such a senseless hoax call were, I don't know, but he got a dressing down from the paramedic for wasting the time of an emergency ambulance crew. And it would be fair justice if the Ketchup proved a little stubborn to clean up afterwards!

Then there's the man who rang treble-nine and threatened suicide, mobilising the police and paramedics to attend his house. It turned out to be a ploy, though, so he could live out his sexual fantasy of having police and ambulance men in uniform in his bedroom. Oh yes, it happened! Though, I can't understand why he assumed male only police and ambulance crews would be dispatched to him!

Then there's the young teenaged girl who, believe it or not, dialled nine, nine, nine to obtain some self-care advice about her minor ailment, because she didn't know the telephone number for the one, one, one service. Incredible! I couldn't help but wonder how she managed to get herself dressed in the morning.

And last but not least, there's the time I was dispatched, as a solo responder on a Rapid Response Vehicle, to a young lady who had sustained a serious laceration to her inner thigh – from a broken wine glass – in a house that was holding a 'ladies only party'. Upon questioning the very slender lass who, bizarrely, had a rather large, taut, bulging belly, about the events leading up to the accident occurring, I asked what her expected 'due date' was. The look of horror and embarrassment on my face after she called me a cheeky sod, and informed me that she wasn't pregnant, must have been a picture to the other twenty or so women in the room! I prayed for the ground to open up and swallow me whole.

How I got out of that address alive, I'll never know! I wouldn't mind if I'd learnt from that mistake, but I didn't; I must have made the same mistake again on at least three separate occasions after that particular incident.

Anyway, I do hope you've enjoyed reading The Lighter Side as much as I enjoyed writing it, and hopefully it has given you a couple of hours of laughter, boosted your immune system, released some endorphins into your circulatory system, or maybe simply provided some escapism from the stress, strain and worry that life often brings. And lest we forget, humour is fun, and free, and it's around us all of the time, it just depends on *your* sense of humour whether you notice it or not!

Bonus Chapter from The Dark Side
Real Life Accounts of an NHS Paramedic
The Good, the Bad and the Downright Ugly

Book Description: Andy Thompson's true-to-life, graphic and gripping account of his work as an NHS paramedic in Britain's A&E emergency Ambulance Service will shock you, sadden you, entertain you, and perhaps inspire you. You'll smile at some of Andy's real patient encounters, while others will cause you to wipe a tear. Using official NHS documentation recorded at the time to give precise details of each incident, Andy has held firm to the real-life accounts, even in keeping the dialogue as close as his memory allows to what was really said at the time. It's as if you're there next to him, struggling with the effects of adrenaline and fighting to save life. This is a rare work of medical non-fiction delivered in a way that is factual, informative, but at the same time naturally entertaining and moving, written with candour and humour. And if you have ever thought what it takes to become a paramedic - or any other of the specialist vocations - and that you could never achieve it yourself, Andy's inspiring story of how he went from postman to frontline healthcare professional, fulfilling his dream, will make you think again that anything is possible if you have the desire. Andy says there are no heroics in the book and that he simply did his job, but we are sure The Dark Side will leave you convinced there are true heroes on our streets right here, right now. Saving lives every day, every night and often against all the odds. It might even change your whole perspective on life.

Baptism of Fire

Just a short time had gone by since I'd finished my paramedic training course, and I was still wet behind the ears, soaking in fact – in terms of paramedic experience, that is. I'd had very little cause to use my new found skills thus far. As an ambulance technician (a paramedic's assistant) I'd experienced the same things as my paramedic peers, granted, but most of the time I had a paramedic to turn to when the shit hit the fan. *I* was now the one that the technician would turn to when the shit hit the fan.

It didn't seem that long ago since I was walking the streets, and donkey's years away from becoming a paramedic. Where had the time gone? It had flown by, that's where, and I'd achieved my ambition, with health care professional registration and paramedic epaulettes to prove it. The responsibility of being the most qualified and skilled member of an ambulance crew, where my clinical decisions could make the difference between life and death, was daunting to say the least, but nonetheless about to begin. And unfortunately for me, the sheer reality of the responsibility I had came in the form of trauma – my *Baptism of Fire*. Allow me to share that experience with you, in considerable detail.

I was approaching the end of a twelve hour night shift on overtime. My crewmate, Adam, a very good friend of mine, was still a rookie; he'd not long transferred to The Dark Side and was still learning his trade as a probationary ambulance technician. Adam was a great character with a fantastic sense of humour, and also an eye for the ladies!

We had not stopped all night, nor had any of the other crews from the same station. We had all been responding to treble-nine after treble-nine, and were absolutely exhausted. We were all sat together in the station mess room chatting and drinking tea. It was 6:45a.m. and we all eagerly awaited our relief staff, who historically would arrive fifteen minutes before the start of their shift. But they had not, so me and Adam were sitting ducks to cop a late treble-nine, as we were the next crew out if an emergency call came in. Another five minutes passed by and there was still no sign of our relief crew. Then, to my disappointment, my hand portable radio sounded.

'Oh, bloody 'ell!' I said, before pressing the push-to-talk button, 'Receiving, over.'

'Roger, RED call to a single vehicle RTC near the junction of

Gaspar Lane. One patient reported; police on route too, over,' the dispatcher said.

'Roger that,' I replied.

Adam and I had no choice but to respond immediately. Now the next crew out were on tenterhooks, as their relief crew had not arrived either. So me and Adam exited the station and adopted our appointed positions in the ambulance – him driving and me in the attendant's seat. As we moved off with blue lights flashing, our relief crew were just getting out of their cars. Adam looked at me with a cunning expression.

'Forget it mate, we'll have to go now,' I said, with temptation to do what Adam was thinking and ask the crew to respond to the RTC for us. I don't know what it was, but I had a sixth sense and thought to myself that it was probably best that we go, as the relief crew were a double technician crew and the incident location had a sixty mile per hour speed limit. This could be very serious and require paramedic intervention.

We drove the three miles to the crash scene, with the blue lights flashing and sirens wailing, chatting along the way but dazed.

'It'll probably be some daft sod with a dent in his car, rubbing his 'ed,' Adam remarked.

'We'll see mate, we'll see,' I replied, less hopeful and an anticipatory sixth sense still lingering. When we rolled up to the scene, a bystander approached the ambulance, so I wound down the window.

'Where's the crash, mate?' I asked.

'Over there,' the bystander said, pointing at a large field.

'Are the police on scene?'

'Yeah, there's a copper with him.'

'OK, cheers mate.'

So me and Adam got out of the ambulance, opened up the side door and grabbed the oxygen and the paramedic bag. While doing

153

that we could see a male lying flat on his back, about twenty-five yards across the field, and a copper kneeling next to him, immobilising his head. But we couldn't see any scene of a collision anywhere, which confused us both. We casually walked towards the patient and the copper, carrying our equipment. From a distance it wasn't clear whether the patient had any injuries or not. As we progressed along the field, we spotted the patient's Subaru to our left; it was a mangled heap of carnage, crunched against a tree.

'It's gonna be a youngster,' I said to Adam, before pausing momentarily. 'Hang on... why isn't he still in the car?' I curiously asked, thinking out aloud but knowing full well Adam would be as clueless as I was. With damage like that, I thought, the occupant should either be dead, trapped or at the very least still inside. It looked like the car had smashed through a fence and come to a sudden halt with the assistance of a tree that must have been hundreds of years old, judging by the size of the trunk. As we got nearer to the patient, an audible sucking sound resonated through my ears. That doesn't sound good, I thought.

'Ohhh shhhit,' I said to Adam with my teeth clenched together in a ventriloquist-like manner. My heart rate more than doubled, from a normal sixty beats per minute (60 bpm) to about one hundred and fifty (150 bpm) within seconds. I could feel it thumping against my chest, as if trying to escape from inside me, and my lungs suddenly demanded more oxygen. Adrenaline was the cause.

I understood adrenaline. Having a broad interest in self-defence and the fighting arts for many years, I'd studied it in some detail, particularly the side effects of it, and also how to control it. But that's the hardest part; it's difficult to control the side effects. If adrenaline is not understood and controlled, it can cause you to freeze on the spot, and panic will set in. The more you panic, the greater the adrenaline release. The greater the adrenaline release, the more you panic. The only way to control adrenaline is to accept its purpose, accept it's there to help you to get through a stressful situation.

154

You see, adrenaline is a hormone produced by the adrenal glands during high stress or exciting situations. This powerful hormone is part of the human body's acute stress response system, also called the 'fight or flight' response. It works by stimulating the heart rate, contracting blood vessels, and dilating air passages, all of which work to increase blood flow to the muscles and oxygen to the lungs. However, adrenaline is often mistaken for fear, not only by the person experiencing the adrenal release, but also by those watching. For instance, during a confrontation or a verbal or physical attack, exposing the effects of adrenaline to your potential attacker is often perceived by *you,* and them, as *you* being scared or weak. But it's as natural as blinking and nothing to be ashamed of or embarrassed about. The assailant will be feeling the same effects too but attempts to hide them with aggressive verbal and mobile body language, such as splaying the arms out to the sides and pacing about to appear bigger and more threatening, thus hiding *his* trembling hands and legs.

Our Neanderthal ancestors would have felt the side effects of adrenaline too, but they would have faced a killer beast, with the odds stacked heavily against them if they didn't run. Now, in the twenty-first century, our bodies consider something as non-life threatening as a driving test as a threat to one's life. So our adrenal glands secrete adrenaline to assist us, to give us the option to either take the driving test (fight), or tell the examiner to shove it up his arse, and then take the bus home instead (flight).

Unfortunately, the side effects of adrenaline do not help under the circumstances often faced by a paramedic. A paramedic cannot choose the flight response; although I have known it to happen at the scene of a cardiac arrest – needless to say, he joined the dole queue!

A paramedic needs to act fast under any circumstances: Adrenaline can cause you to freeze on the spot, practically glue you to the floor.

A paramedic needs to think on his feet: Oxygen is drawn away from the brain, causing confusion.

A paramedic needs to be able to listen to what is being said: Environmental deafness often occurs.

A paramedic needs to be able to ask questions and give out clear instructions to his crewmate and other emergency services: A dry, pasty mouth can cause a tremor in the voice.

A paramedic needs steady hands to be able to carefully and accurately put a needle into a patient's vein (cannulation), or a tube down their windpipe (intubation): Adrenaline causes the hands to sweat and shake like crazy.

It's bizarre. Here I was, a picture of health – compared to this poor sod anyway, who was absolutely covered in blood – and my body responded as if it was *my* life in danger. Fortunately I understood adrenaline and knew to accept it and control it through diaphragmatic breathing.

Diaphragmatic breathing helps close down the sympathetic nervous system, which is responsible for speeding *things* up in the body. Diaphragmatic breathing shuts off the fear; it switches off the adrenaline release. When you take deep breaths you fool the brain in to thinking that the 'threat' to your life has gone. Obviously there was no threat to me, but like I said, our body perceives even a driving test to be a threat to life. The other very important aspect of understanding adrenaline is learning to hide it; you can't entirely, but it is possible. By doing so, the patient doesn't perceive you to be panicking.

Most people do not understand adrenaline; they view the side effects as fear and then begin to panic. If a patient notices the paramedic panicking then the patient, or the patient's friends or loved ones watching, are likely to begin panicking too, assuming that if the paramedic is panicking, something must be seriously wrong. However, working at speed is not the same as panicking; it is simply recognising that time is of the essence, and understanding that seconds save lives.

Anyway, let's get back to the scene.

When we reached the patient's side, I acknowledged the copper but was immediately drawn to the 'claret' soaking the entire front of the casualty's unzipped bomber jacket and his t-shirt, which was dripping, from his yet to be fully identified wounds, on to the grass. I knelt down next to him, the adrenaline continuing to course through my veins like a steam train; but I'd learnt how to remain calm on the outside, like a duck gliding along the surface of a pond, even though on the inside my heart was going ten to the dozen, like a duck's little webbed feet underwater. I gazed at his face and was astonished by the sheer pallor of his skin; he was grey, sweaty and extremely clammy to the touch. I then looked at his chest, quickly noticing that every time he breathed, his t-shirt concaved inwards while a rapid sucking noise could be heard. So I took a deep breath and, as calmly as possible, began ascertaining some details from him.

'What's y'name, mate?' I asked, trying to hide the little tremor in my voice. His eyes were closed but he opened them when he heard my voice, and muttered what I heard to be Jason, but it sounded incomprehensible. Nevertheless, I was able to assess and confirm his conscious level as 'responds to verbal stimuli'.

In the medical profession, the 'AVPU' scale is used to quickly assess a patient's consciousness level:

'A' is 'Alert'.

'V' is 'responds to Verbal stimuli'.

'P' is 'responds to Painful stimuli'.

'U' is 'Unresponsive to any stimuli'.

Based on his AVPU, I quickly took out a nasopharyngeal airway adjunct (a narrow tube made of soft, malleable plastic) from the paramedic bag, applied KY jelly to it, and inserted it with a twisting motion into his right nostril. This would ensure a patent airway in the event his conscious level reduced further, causing him to be unable to maintain his own airway. The fact that he tolerated a tube inserted into his nose was secondary confirmation that he had a lowered conscious level. I then applied an oxygen mask to his face and administered high flow oxygen to him.

With Adam stood by my side, initially redundant, I took hold of Jason's wrist to feel for a radial pulse, and to check for the rate of his pulse too. The presence of a radial pulse signifies a systolic blood pressure of *at least* eighty millimetres of mercury, or 80mmHg, although textbook figures vary. A normal adult 'textbook' systolic blood pressure would be one hundred and twenty millimetres of mercury, or 120mmHg. A systolic below 90mmHg is considered low blood pressure.

Systolic means the arterial pressure during contraction of the heart. It is measured in 'millimetres of mercury', pertaining to the fact that sphygmomanometers – the equipment used for measuring blood pressure – historically contained mercury, hence the letters 'mmHg' following the preceding figure. The use of mercury sphygmomanometers is no longer common practice amongst health care professionals around the globe, and has generally been replaced with digital instruments, and aneroid types that have a dial. Palpating a radial pulse is merely an approximate measurement prior to actually measuring a patient's blood pressure.

Jason didn't have a palpable radial pulse, so I checked for a central pulse (i.e. the carotid pulse in his neck). He had one. That indicated to me that his systolic blood pressure was at least 60mmHg, but at that level it would be life threateningly low! Given the absence of a palpable radial pulse, I could only assume – by the state of Jason's car and how he was presenting in my primary 'Airway, Breathing and Circulation' (ABC) survey – that his blood pressure was 'in his boots'. He was in hypovolaemic shock caused by a low volume of blood. His vital organs were not being adequately perfused due to an insufficient amount of oxygenated blood circulating the body. He was shutting down right in front of me and would soon die without invasive action.

I pressed hard on the nail bed of his right hand, which caused Jason to pull away. Then, I rapidly made a mental calculation of his Glasgow Coma Score, or GCS. To keep it really simple, a GCS is a number from three to fifteen based on a patient's consciousness level – which can fluctuate, both up and down, throughout an assessment and treatment. Anything lower than fifteen is classed as a reduced level of consciousness; Jason's GCS was nine. He scored three for responding to my voice, a two for making incomprehensible sounds, and a four for withdrawing from painful stimuli when I pressed hard on the nail bed of his right hand. A GCS of nine was poor to say the least.

Adam was stood beside me, taken aback by Jason's presentation. The copper, still holding Jason's head, looked directly at me,

'What do you want me to do, mate?' he asked, with a look of alarm on his face. Almost simultaneously, Adam gazed at me with a helpless expression and said,

'What do you want mate?' Reality kicked in. I thought where's the paramedic I was used to looking to for support, where is he? He's not here.

My paramedic course flashed before my eyes. I'd practiced critical trauma scenarios countless times just weeks ago; this was now the real thing. I took a couple of deep breaths, right from the bottom of the diaphragm. The trauma knowledge came flooding to the front of my brain, ready to implement. Time was of the essence because Jason had time-critical features, and the outcome would depend on how quick I initiated his assessment and treatment, and got him to a trauma centre.

In a trauma setting there are terms called the Golden Hour and the Platinum Ten. The Golden Hour means that if an unstable patient with time-critical features is being assessed and treated in hospital, preferably a trauma centre, within an hour from the time of the incident, then the prognosis is far better than if they are not in hospital within the hour.

The Platinum Ten is the number of minutes – from arriving at the patient's side to being mobile to hospital – it should preferably take a paramedic to assess and provide initial treatment to a seriously injured trauma patient. It can be done, and was done on numerous occasions during trauma scenarios just several weeks previous, on my paramedic course. However, it's not always that simple in real life as it is in training.

Adam and the copper were awaiting a response.

'Right, you keep holding his head and keep talking to him, that's it!' I said to the copper.

'Adam, you get the scoop stretcher, head-blocks, Velcro straps and a rigid collar. No spider straps! We haven't got time to put the spider straps on. He's time-critical, so we'll have to sacrifice full immobilisation to save his life.' The copper remained where he was, holding Jason's head. Adam ran off towards the ambulance to fetch the equipment I had requested. I pulled out my tuffcut scissors and started cutting Jason's t-shirt off, from the bottom upwards, leaving his unzipped bomber jacket in place. When I reached the top of the t-shirt and opened out the sides and exposed his upper body, there was a huge hole in the right-hand side of his chest, the size of two adult hands. The majority of the right side of his chest and ribcage had been obliterated by a brutal outside force that had barely ripped his t-shirt on impact. I could visibly see his right lung, which had also sustained severe damage.

The sucking noise was caused by a large fold of skin tissue, flapping as environmental air entered and escaped the large space in his chest with each rapid breath. And now the t-shirt was cut open, it became very clear that this young lad was not long for this earth. Adrenaline continued to hurtle through my veins, and the inside of my chest felt like a boxer was using my heart as a speed ball – B'dum-B'dum-B'dum-B'dum-B'dum-B'dum-B'dum-B'dum-B'dum. I'm sure I could hear my own heartbeat over the whistling of the surrounding sparrows. I accepted it was adrenaline and I would not allow it to cause me to panic. It was there to help me get through this ordeal. So, once again I took a couple of deep breaths to fool my brain into believing the threat had gone. I opened up some large ambulance dressings, placing them, unfolded, over the huge, gaping, haemorrhaging chest wound, to keep it as clean as possible.

Again, I asked Jason his name, age and other distracting questions; I hadn't forgotten his name, I was just assessing to see if his

160

AVPU had reduced from a 'V' to a 'P' or a 'U'. I cut the right-hand sleeve of his bomber jacket and applied a tourniquet to his arm, and then began rummaging through the paramedic bag for a cannula; a needle that you insert into a vein, leaving a clear plastic tube in place to administer drugs or fluids, or sometimes both. I chose the largest diameter cannula that paramedics carry; it is a wide needle, primarily used for life threatening trauma injuries, and it was safe to say that it was a good time to use one. Jason was so shut down that even the tourniquet was not engorging any veins in his arm.

With my heart still going like the clappers, I took several deep breaths to try and control the adrenaline from causing my hands to shake. I patted his arm where a vein should physiologically be and pierced the skin with the needle, practically cannulating blindfold. Jason tried to pull his arm away when the needle pierced his skin, but I was restraining his arm for that very reason. I was praying for blood to appear in the flashback chamber, which usually confirms successful intravenous access. The flashback appeared, so I advanced the needle further and awaited a secondary flashback to appear along the length of the clear plastic tube. The secondary flashback appeared.

'Nice one, I'm in,' I said to the copper, followed by a deep sigh of relief.

With an evident flashback, I unclipped the tourniquet, applied digital (thumb) pressure to the vein, withdrew the needle and discarded the needle into the sharps container, leaving the clear plastic tube inside his vein. I screwed the Luer-Lock to the end and quickly secured it in place with an adhesive dressing, before flushing it with a pre-filled, ten-millilitre syringe of sodium chloride to confirm patent 'IV access' – he was going to need it! With 'IV access' secured, I turned to the copper,

'What 'appened 'ere anyway?' I asked with my mind racing, waiting for Adam to return. 'And why is he so far away from the car?'

'The bloke over there witnessed it. He said he lost control on the

161

bend, crashed through the fence, and then crashed into that tree. So he ran over and pulled him out of the car and laid him here. A piece of timber smashed through the windscreen and staked his chest,' the copper explained.

'Bloody 'ell,' I said, shaking my head with disbelief that he was still alive.

Adam returned with the equipment. He positioned the scoop on to the ground, separated it and placed one half either side of Jason. That's the beauty of the scoop, it separates in two, and then each part can be slid underneath the patient and clipped back together, forming a stretcher. With the copper still immobilising Jason's head, I placed the collar around his neck, then with Adam used a synchronised rolling method and positioned each half of the scoop underneath Jason, before clipping the two ends together. I then put a head-block on each side of his head and secured them in place with Velcro straps. As we were doing that, much to my relief, Danny, an experienced paramedic in an RRV (Rapid Response Vehicle) rolled up on blue lights. I wasn't looking to him for advice – I was coping well – so before he even had chance to place one foot on the grass, I turned and stared at him with what must have looked like madman eyes, and shouted,

'Danny, get me a litre of fluid set up, now!'

He immediately, without hesitation, leapt on to our ambulance and began to set up the bag of fluid I had less than politely requested. The fluid I was going to use – sodium chloride – doesn't have oxygen carrying capabilities like blood has, it merely increases the volume of fluid in the body's circulatory system. Nonetheless, it can improve the prognosis in a hypovolaemic patient.

As we had now placed Jason onto the scoop stretcher, we then, between me, Adam and the copper, lifted him across the twenty-five yards of the field to the ambulance and placed the scoop onto the ambulance stretcher. I quickly attached the fluid administration equipment that Danny had prepared, known as a 'fluid giving set', to the cannula in Jason's arm and opened up the clamp so fluid would run rapidly through his veins. This was intended to increase his blood pressure to the point he had a palpable radial pulse, thus confirming a systolic blood pressure of at least 80mmHg. However, as the body has a natural defence mechanism to clot haemorrhaging, administering fluid can encourage clots to dilute and break down, therefore causing haemorrhaging to recommence – if haemorrhaging has ceased – or it can reduce the body's own natural clotting factors from functioning. That was a consideration I had to take into account when I opened up the clamp and infused fluid into Jason. I didn't have a lot of choice though. His blood pressure was so low that he would die without, what we call in the medical profession, a 'fluid challenge'.

'Right, Adam, get on to ambulance control and tell 'em to alert A 'n' E. I want a full trauma team including anaesthetist. Tell 'em RTC versus fence and tree, in that order. Driver nineteen years old, GCS nine, open sucking chest wound. Tell 'em to request 'O' negative blood t'be on standby. Do it now!' I said, with clear instruction in my voice.

'OK mate,' Adam replied.

I felt for a palpable radial pulse again; he still didn't have one. I wasn't expecting one yet, I was just being impatient, so I allowed the fluid to keep draining from the hanging drip into his veins. I shone my pen torch into each of his pupils to assess that they were both equal in size and reactive to light. That does not necessarily rule out a head injury, but is a positive sign if the pupils are equal and reactive to light. Fortunately, Jason's pupils were normal, but based on the state of his car crunched against the tree, a head injury could not be ruled out, yet.

While periodically feeling for a radial pulse in his wrist, I continued to cut off the rest of his clothes, from his socks and trainers upwards, in order to completely expose his body, with the exception of his underwear for dignity purposes. When I started cutting the body of the bomber jacket off, it became apparent that it was filled with feathers, and because of the breeze flowing through the open rear doors of the ambulance, the feathers went everywhere; floating around the saloon, landing in his open wounds, landing in the blood on his body and into the blood that had dripped on to the floor from his open chest wound and other less serious haemorrhaging injuries. I needed the jacket off though, to expose the whole of his upper body so the doctors could undertake a rapid secondary survey; that is look, listen and feel for other injuries on the body in addition to the obvious injuries he had. Then I covered him with several blankets to keep him warm, as he was by now practically as naked as the day he was born.

Adam had conveyed a pre-alert message to the ambulance dispatcher, who would pass on the information to the receiving hospital's A&E department. He then closed the rear and side doors, adopted his position in the driver's seat and began mobilising on blue lights to hospital, which was only a few miles away. I took hold of Jason's wrist and felt for a palpable radial pulse. He still didn't have one.

'Bloody 'ell, he's lost a bucket full,' I thought. I gazed at his chest as the wound continued to make a sucking sound every time he breathed in and out. Then, all of a sudden, Jason spoke,

'Am I gonna die?' He paused momentarily. 'Am I gonna die? I've gotta girlfriend,' he mumbled, at the same time opened his eyes.

'You just keep talkin' to me Jason, you're gonna be fine,' I said, attempting to reassure him. 'Your name is Jason, isn't it?'

'Uh... think,' he confusedly muttered. I didn't know what else to say. I couldn't exactly reply with yes, probably mate, you've got bloody awful injuries so there's very little chance you're going to survive... could I! However, because he had asked me a question with his eyes open, without any verbal or painful stimuli from me, meant that his GCS had increased from nine to twelve; probably due to the IV fluid and oxygen I'd administered having a positive effect on his circulation, thus causing more oxygenated blood to travel to his brain. By now, 800 millilitres of fluid had infused through the cannula in his arm. So I felt for a radial pulse again, and there was one; excellent I thought. It was weak but nonetheless palpable. The fluid had worked. It had increased his blood pressure to a level adequate enough to buy him time for the real lifesavers to go to work on him. I adjusted the clamp so the fluid infusion reduced to a very steady drip, because I didn't want to increase his blood pressure too much.

Throughout the journey to hospital, all I did was periodically monitor the amount of fluid draining from the hanging drip, and hold his wrist to make sure he maintained a radial pulse and to give him some assurance that someone was there with him. I didn't measure his oxygen saturations, better known as *sats* or *SP02*, which is a measurement of how well oxygenated the blood is in the body. I didn't undertake a single measurement of his blood pressure, blood glucose or even analyse an ECG to see what his exact heart rate and rhythm was. It didn't matter. This guy needed doctors; an A&E consultant, an anaesthetist and a surgeon to be precise, not a paramedic playing around on scene, ticking all the boxes to meet the criteria for pre-hospital trauma found in a textbook. The basic paramedic skill of high flow oxygen administration, a cannula and a fluid challenge was keeping him alive.

As we approached the hospital, I reassured Jason that we were nearly there; by 'there' I meant the place he needed to be if he stood any chance of survival, although I obviously didn't say that to him. When we eventually arrived at A&E – it felt like a lifetime even though it had only been several minutes – Adam parked up in the ambulance bay, vacated his seat, and quickly opened the rear doors and lowered the ramp. A trauma team had gathered in the entrance doorway, awaiting the patient they had been put on alert for; they were all gloved and gowned ready to pounce on the poor sod. We wheeled the stretcher inside and quickly lifted the scoop onto the resuscitation bed.

The room was by now swarming with medical staff, and an appointed lead doctor was awaiting my handover. As paramedics are usually the first health care professionals on scene and hold vital information about an incident, a doctor usually listens to a handover from the paramedic while other doctors commence the assessment and treatment of the sick or injured patient. In this case, for instance, information on the extent of the damage to the vehicle, what the approximate speed of impact was, and what injuries have been sustained, to name but a few. A handover is intended to summarise the history of events and observations undertaken by the paramedic, and the treatment provided. A handover is not usually conveyed grammatically or in full sentences, because doing so prolongs the process; if you have requested the resuscitation room, then the doctor needs information fast! Therefore, a handover is usually passed without interruption from anyone else in the resuscitation room.

I must emphasise that handovers do not always flow in as structured a way as you would like them to. Sometimes you forget some of the information that would be beneficial to the A&E consultant, due to the extent of the observations ascertained and the treatment you have provided. It is an acquired skill, and I'm not afraid to admit that I'm still trying to improve my handover technique to the present day.

For the benefit of the layperson, I have simplified handovers throughout this book. Therefore my handover went something like this:

'Right, this is Jason. Approximately nineteen years old. Jason was a single occupant of a Subaru driving approximately sixty mile per hour. Jason crashed through a fence; sudden halt on impact with a large tree trunk at 0650 hours. Seatbelt worn.

'Jason was pulled from the car by a bystander. On arrival he was lay flat on his back and a police officer was immobilising c-spine. Airway patent but nasal airway inserted and tolerated. AVPU initially V. GCS initially nine, but increased to twelve on route. Rapid shallow respiratory rate, O2 administered. No initial palpable radial pulse. He was grey, sweaty and clammy.

'On examination, huge open, sucking chest wound caused by a wooden stake through the windscreen; which I've covered as best as I could. Mechanism of injury cannot rule out spinal, pelvic or head injury. Pupils equal and reactive to light.

'No sats. No blood pressure. No blood glucose. No ECG

monitored, and only partial immobilisation applied due to him presenting with life threatening, time-critical features. Patient's clothes cut off but no opportunity to do secondary survey.

'Large bore IV cannula inserted into the right arm, and just over eight hundred millilitres of fluid administered to restore a palpable radial pulse, which I have confirmed as present on route and on arrival here at A&E.

'Are there any questions?'

'No, thank you... well done,' the doctor replied, looking alternately between me and Jason.

Within a few minutes of arriving at A&E, Jason had been anaesthetised, intubated and manually ventilated by the anaesthetist. He was also catheterised, had another large bore cannula inserted into his left arm, his blood pressure and blood glucose measured, and had also been attached to an ECG monitor. He was in good hands and plenty of them.

It's amazing what can be done when there are more than two medical professionals available to attempt to stabilise a dying patient. All I had done was keep his blood pressure up with IV fluid, which bought him valuable time, and then scoop and run to the nearest hospital. The incident had gone smooth, and we had achieved the Golden Hour and the Platinum Ten too.

Adam and I then went outside to deeply inhale some much needed air, leaving the doctors to work on trying to stabilise Jason. We both gazed into the back of the ambulance through the open rear doors; it was an absolute mess, with feathers, equipment, packaging and blood everywhere, on the floor, up the walls, on the cupboard doors. It looked like ten chickens had been slaughtered. I looked down at my uniform to find more blood on me than an abattoir's floor; I'd paid no attention to how blood-soiled I'd become while treating Jason.

I started the paperwork while Adam had an attempt at cleaning up the mess in the ambulance to restore it to an acceptable standard, prior to its inevitable deep clean by a private, infection control valeting company. There was no doubt that it was coming off the road and out of service for the rest of the day.

We should have finished our shift at 7 a.m. but we only cleared from hospital at 9 a.m. Once my paperwork was complete, the ambulance clean (cleanish anyway), and our job done, we headed on back to the station. Throughout the twenty minute journey, we barely said a word to each other, probably due to tiredness of what was now becoming nearly a fifteen hour non-stop shift; and also because we were both still a little stunned from what we had just experienced.

When we arrived back at the station there was nobody about. We had taken so long at hospital, completing paperwork and cleaning the ambulance, that our relief crew had taken a spare ambulance and gone out on stand-by, or to a treble-nine or urgent call. Adam and I went into the changing room and carefully removed our blood-stained uniforms, being careful not to touch the claret-soaked areas, and then placed the lot into a clinical waste bag, ready for the furnace. There was no point in trying to salvage uniform; we had plenty of it for incidents that involved getting covered in excessive bodily fluids. We scrubbed up, put our 'civvies' on, had a quick chat and then went our separate ways to our awaiting beds.

By the time I arrived home, I had been awake for so long that I'd started getting a second stamina and didn't want to go to bed. So I sat on the couch with a cup of tea, reminiscing over the job. It suddenly dawned on me why Mr X – my paramedic instructor – had been so relentless; it was necessary in order to cope with incidents like the one Adam and I had just dealt with. And without all that intense training, study and all those character testing fictitious scenarios, I honestly don't think I'd have been able to handle it, let alone take charge.

Later that night, back on night shift duty, after I'd handed over a patient to the nurse in A&E, I asked the A&E consultant who had cared for Jason what had happened to him. He informed me that he remained in a critical condition and had been transferred to the

Cardiothoracic Centre later that day, where both in and out-patients go for heart (cardio) and chest (thoracic) related diagnosis, treatment or surgery.

I very rarely went to the Cardiothoracic Centre, so was unable to find out what happened to Jason. It is often very difficult for paramedics to follow-up their patients' diagnosis, continuing treatment or outcome once they have been handed over to A&E. Patients are either admitted to a ward, discharged or, like Jason, transferred to another hospital, and you cannot just ring up the hospital and ask how a patient is doing, because you could be anyone. They won't just take your word for it that you're the paramedic who dealt with a particular patient you're enquiring about.

However, six months later I conveyed an elderly patient to the Cardiothoracic Centre for a routine out-patient appointment. So, while I was there, I couldn't resist the temptation to ask the receptionist if she could check on the patient data system for information if I gave her Jason's full name, which I had remembered with ease, and although not strictly permissible, she obliged. I also gave her some background information as to what had happened and what injuries Jason had sustained on that adrenal-fuelled morning. The receptionist, shocked and intrigued at the story, browsed the system for his details. I waited in anticipation, and after a bit of swift keyboard tapping, she found his records.

'Did he make it? Did he survive?' I asked impatiently, leaning over the reception desk. She looked up at me and smiled,

'Yeah, he's been discharged and has a routine follow-up appointment in six months.'

'No way! That's excellent, nice one!' I replied, with a beaming grin on my face.

I couldn't believe it. With the injuries he had sustained, nobody would have believed he could have possibly survived long enough for surgeons to go to work on him, but by some miracle he had.

Although he would have to live with *huge* physical scars – and no doubt mental scars too – that would remind him of that very day and those horrendous injuries that he sustained, for the rest of his life.

Available in Paperback, Digital and Audio Download

The Dark Side

Real Life Accounts of an NHS Paramedic

The Good, the Bad and the Downright Ugly

Please continue reading to sample a

Bonus Chapter from The Dark Side Part 2

Real Life Accounts of an NHS Paramedic

The Traumatic, the Tragic and the Tearful

Book Description: Following up on his well-received first book, Andy Thompson provides another captivating, thought-provoking and at times intense glimpse into the daily life of a Paramedic working in the UK's National Health Service. In the style of his first book, Andy recalls each event from the detailed documentation recorded at the time, each account written in a way that puts the reader right there next to him so that you live the events in realtime, hear the dialogue between paramedics, patient, their loved ones and other healthcare professionals as it would have been, and share in Andy's thought processes during each of the ten very different situations he encounters.

The term 'The Dark Side' describes the frontline emergency aspect of the Ambulance Service, since paramedics frequently experience sombre situations. In 'The Dark Side, Part 2' you will share in some truly traumatic, tragic and tearful events involving a seemingly vibrant, healthy young patient, a prison inmate, the victims of an horrific car crash, heart attacks, a frightening epileptic fit, the alarming effects of an allergic reaction, and what can happen when under-strain doctors prescribe the wrong medication. But there's still room for lighthearted moments and a taste of the sometimes dark humour that allows paramedics to continually deal with events most of us would find too horrific.

The detail in the descriptions of the care given to each patient on-scene by Andy and his colleagues will have you marvelling at the ability of these healthcare professionals to work at such speed of thought, buying enough time to deliver a patient into the specialist hands of hospital care and often full recovery. Of course there are inevitably also those times when tears of hope turn to tears of despair for loved ones. You cannot feel that pain until it happens to you, but this book will bring you mighty close to it at times.

Blackout

We're very fortunate in the UK that the NHS operates twenty-four-seven, three hundred and sixty-five days of the year. Granted, summer is the best part of the year for paramedics because we occasionally get to relax in the sun and sit on standby, 'people watching', while eating an ice-cream; fantastic! Though, I've had to dispose of a lot of ice-creams prematurely in order to promptly respond to an emergency call. Spring and autumn are not too bad either, but winter, however, can be hell! It's freezing cold on a day shift, even colder on a night shift, and when it snows, good grief! Mother Nature cuts the emergency services no slack whatsoever.

Regardless of poor weather conditions, people obviously get sick and have accidents and subsequently ring treble-nine. Winter weather can sometimes make the job of ambulance crews very difficult. There are increased risks associated with driving, and with access and egress to and from patients' homes, particularly egressing, as carrying patients in the carry-chair down snow covered or frozen-over concrete steps, driveways and pavements, etcetera, is often very daunting. I've known many accidents to happen, some of which resulted in ambulance personnel getting injured badly enough to have no choice but to go on long-term sickness leave. Nevertheless, it's a risk that ambulance personnel have to take to help patients who need us at their worst hour, as the following patient did in the early hours of a cold winter morning while I was on a night shift.

It was 2:40 a.m. and it had been snowing for most of the night, and it still was. There was a good few inches of snow spread like a blanket all over the grounds of the ambulance station and beyond. I was on station in the mess room, power-napping, sat with three of my colleagues, including fellow paramedic and my crewmate, Adele. The night had been quite busy thus far and I was beginning to wilt a bit through sheer exhaustion. My brain did not feel ready to be taxed for the remainder of the shift. I began feeling a little restless and therefore decided to go outside for some fresh air and to admire the crisp, white snow. Actually, as I've mentioned snow, I'll have to tell you a little humorous anecdote a former colleague told me when I was working as a postman. It went something like this.

Before my friend was a postman, he worked for a well-known brewery. Upon him finishing a night shift at seven o'clock in the morning, he clocked-off along with his work mates and exited the premises, and although he knew it had been snowing, he was surprised to see it had snowed as much as it had, so much in fact that he was able to make decent sized snowballs. While several of his colleagues had an early morning snowball fight, he walked towards his car parked on the roadside, talking to a female colleague as he strolled along, casually picking up snow as they conversed. When he arrived at his car he said goodbye and parted from her.

She continued to amble towards her car a short distance away. As she got into her car, her back to my friend, he threw a snowball in her direction. Proceeding to slam the car door shut, some snow went into the foot-well. Not knowing who had thrown it, and without observing for any passing vehicles, she abruptly opened the door to remove the snow from inside her car. At the same time, another car drove past on her side of the road. BANG! The passing car took her door clean off its hinges. Having heard the bang and the shocked woman's scream, her colleagues, including my friend, went over to help and calm her. However, to the present day he has never told her that it was him who threw the snowball. I absolutely love it when would-be harmless pranks go wrong; it makes them all the funnier.

Anyway, after standing outside for ten minutes watching the snow fall heavily, and having inhaled some fresh air, I went back into the mess room and offered to make tea. I often make tea while on station just for the sake of it, because you never know when, or even where your next cup is coming from. I do occasionally accept the offer of a brew in a patient's house, but only if I can assess and treat them at home… and as long as they're not mingers!

I entered the kitchen. If it had been a very busy previous seventy-two hours or so for the crews, it sometimes resembled the kitchen from the politically incorrect, yet hilarious UK sitcom *The Young Ones*. So I began the challenge of looking for clean cups that didn't have deep tannin stains embedded, or Penicillin growing inside them. I'm serious! I don't know if it's just the ambulance service or all of the emergency services, but trying to find clean crockery in the station kitchen is like looking for a virgin in a maternity ward.

So, stood alone in the kitchen, I ascertained my fellow colleagues' tea preferences. And as per usual, ascertaining tea preferences from the crew I was working with that particular night would have gone something like this:

'How do you want yours, Bill?' I'd shout through to the mess room.

'Julie Andrews for me please, Andy,' he'd say, meaning 'white nun'. 'Don't make it fortnight tea though, will you.' By that he meant not too weak.

'OK, how about you, Adele?' I'd ask.

'Arnie please,' she'd say, meaning she wanted hers strong. Who would think you could speak in code making a simple cup of tea, hey!

I didn't get a chance to make a brew because Adele and I were dispatched to a fifty-seven year old male complaining of chest pain, before I'd even had the chance to finish washing the cups to an acceptable state to drink from. We promptly vacated the station and Adele drove towards the address given to us, using blue lights, but she refrained from using the sirens. Due to the poor weather conditions, Adele had little choice but to drive slowly, and to gently navigate around bends and use deceleration to slow down, as opposed to frequent use of the brakes, to minimise the risk of skidding.

When we arrived at the address, we grabbed the bare essential

174

equipment only, not because we were being lazy but because chest pain is better assessed and treated in the ambulance; we therefore intended to get the patient into the ambulance as soon as possible. Between us both, we carried the Entonox – a.k.a 'gas and air' – a carry-chair, two blankets and the ECG machine and walked towards the house along the snow covered driveway.

The ECG machine can not only be used to analyse a patient's heart rhythm, but can be used to 'shock' – or defibrillate, to be precise – a patient who goes in to cardiac arrest, providing that they present in one of two arrhythmias where defibrillation is an appropriate form of medical intervention; that is Ventricular Fibrillation (VF) or *Pulseless* Ventricular Tachycardia (VT). I say *pulseless* because a person can present with VT but have a pulse and be fully conscious, and therefore does not meet the criteria for defibrillation.

When we arrived at the front door, we were welcomed by a lady, the patient's wife. She escorted us to the large lounge where the patient, George, was sat down on the sofa, dressed in his PJ's. I took one look at him and thought, 'Heart Attack!' Amongst other tell-tale signs, he was holding his clenched fist close to his chest. That single gesture of body language put my diagnostic senses on heightened alert, because that is a typical sign of someone experiencing crushing-like chest pain.

Chest pain is a cardinal sign of a heart attack, or myocardial infarction (MI), to be precise. However, chest pain can also be the sign of numerous other conditions, some life-threatening and others not so life-threatening. Nevertheless, when someone rings treble-nine and mentions chest pain, the caller is questioned from the highest acuity to the lowest acuity, but in most cases an ambulance is dispatched immediately – regardless of the patient's age – just in case it is a heart attack that is causing the patient's chest pain.

Looking directly at George, I immediately noticed his face was ashen and he was sweating profusely. His facial expression was that of someone frightened to death... no, frightened *of* death

175

would be a better description. That is known in medical textbooks as 'a fear of impending doom', and it's a very unpleasant sight to witness, let alone be the person actually feeling it. His breathing was quite shallow, partly due to anxiety, but perhaps more so due to his struggling heart trying to provide enough oxygenated blood to the vital organs of his body. Adele and I looked at each other, instantly acknowledging George's death-like appearance. His presentation caused me to get ahead of myself a little and I started to think about all the basic and advanced skills and observations that we were going to have to do, on top of a myriad of drugs we would need to administer if my suspicions were correct. And they would need undertaking fast. 'I want him in the ambulance A-S-A-P!' I thought.

I sat down on the sofa next to George and applied a pair of disposable, protective nitrile gloves. Remaining calm, with Adele and George's wife stood beside me, I introduced myself and Adele. Then, using implied consent, I took hold of his wrist to feel for an approximate rate and strength of his pulse. While doing that, I could feel he was very sweaty and clammy to the touch; in fact, that's an understatement, he was wringing wet through, his pyjama top was clinging to his body like Lycra. With his initial presentation mentally noted, I then began to ascertain some pertinent history from him, with regards to the background events that had resulted in a treble-nine call being made.

'George, you're holding your chest, I take it you still have chest pain, is that right?' I asked, knowing full well what his answer would be, but didn't want to assume.

'Yeah,' he replied, with a look of fear on his face and sweat dripping down his pale forehead.

As George still had pain, I immediately asked Adele to get me a *sats*, also known as *SP02*, which is placed on a digit, usually the index finger, to measure how well the blood circulating around the body is being oxygenated. It also attempts to display a pulse rate, although the pulse measurement is rarely accurate. Normal saturations of oxygen would be between ninety-five and one

176

hundred percent on atmospheric air. While Adele waited for George's sats to display, I asked her to prepare and hand over the Entonox to him to self-administer of his own free will. Entonox is an analgesic usually offered to women in labour, but is also frequently used as an initial pain relief for chest pain, or other pain such as limb fractures, until IV access is obtained. Then, if appropriate, a more potent intravenous analgesic can be administered in addition to Entonox.

George began self-administering the Entonox while I continued to palpate the rate and strength of his pulse. It felt slow and weak. That concerned me a lot and caused me to consider deviating slightly from the normal procedure undertaken for a patient with chest pain, particularly a heart attack; that is, until I could confirm whether my suspicions were correct or not. I pondered for a moment, 'What if George is having a heart attack, where is the occlusion? His pulse is slow and weak. What if it is in the inferior (lower) part of his heart; that would mean certain drugs might make his condition even worse.' What I needed was a blood pressure and an ECG to enable me to select and administer the right treatment to George. Directing my gaze at Adele, I asked,

'Can you take his blood pressure, hun?' Then I glanced back at George and asked, 'What time did the pain come on, George?' Momentarily releasing his lips from the Entonox mouthpiece, he answered,

'About an hour ago, it woke me up.'

'OK, does anything improve the pain, like leaning forward?' I asked. George leant forward,

'No,' he said, before inhaling on the Entonox again.

'Does anything make the pain worse, like taking a deep breath in?' He took an exaggerated deep breath, which is what I wanted him to do.

'No,' he answered.

'How would you describe the pain: dull, tight, crushing?' I asked with relevance.

'Crushing, like someone is hugging me too hard.'

'And does the pain radiate anywhere?'

'Down my arm and in my jaw,' he answered, rubbing the palm of his right hand down his left arm.

Pain down the arm, particularly the left arm, and in the jaw is a common complaint from a patient suffering from a heart attack; although that can also be a typical complaint of a cardiac condition called angina. That is where the blood flow to the heart via a coronary artery is partially restricted, as opposed to being completely restricted, as in a *typical* heart attack. Angina can be a pre-cursor to a full-blown heart attack, particularly if the angina-like pain comes on at rest. However, if angina pain comes on during mild exertion, it is commonly treated by the patient with a drug called Glycerol Tri-nitrate, or GTN for short. GTN is a potent vasodilator, which means when sprayed under the patient's tongue it causes arteries to dilate, thus allowing an adequate amount of oxygenated blood to flow to the heart.

Due to George complaining of pain in the jaw and down his arm, and that it had come on at rest, I was becoming more and more convinced that he was having a heart attack and so proceeded to treat him for one. Still sat beside him on the sofa, I continued to question him further.

'George, can you take aspirin, you're not allergic to it are you? Or do you have any active gastric ulcers, or are you on any blood thinners such as warfarin?'

'No, I can take aspirin,' he answered in a breathless manner. So I removed an aspirin from its packaging and handed it to George to chew, then progressed with my initial assessment and treatment for a suspected, but as yet unconfirmed, heart attack.

'Now, on a scale of zero to ten, ten being the worst pain you have ever been in, how would you score the crushing chest pain that you have right now?'

'Ten,' he said with clear certainty.

'Do you feel nauseas at all, or have you vomited since the pain came on?'

'No,' he said, shaking his head, still with the 'fear of impending doom' expression on his face.

Following that questioning, my suspicions had risen even further. Based on his ashen and sweaty appearance and his answers, I was pretty confident that George was having a heart attack. If my suspicions were correct, he could deteriorate to a cardiac arrest within minutes and I didn't want that happening while we were in the house. Actually, I didn't want that to happen at all! But if it did, as previously mentioned, carrying patients in the carry-chair down snow covered or frozen-over concrete steps is often very daunting, but carrying a 'dead weight' from the house in the snow and ice is fraught with danger and a whole lot more difficult than with a 'live' patient. Plus, because the ground was layered with snow, it would make wheeling the carry-chair across the driveway to the ambulance a lot more difficult too.

George was a time-critical patient and needed to receive the appropriate pre-hospital treatment and conveying to hospital fast!

'Right, do you have any other medical conditions at all, George?'

'He's diabetic,' his wife answered before George even had chance to.

'Do you take insulin, George?'

'Yeah... It's in the fridge if you need it,' his wife answered again, as if performing a ventriloquist act with her husband.

'No, that's fine,' I said to her, before directing my eyes at Adele,

'What's his blood pressure, hun?'

'One hundred over sixty, and his sats are ninety-six percent on gas 'n' air. The sats monitor is showing a pulse rate of fifty,' she replied.

'Cheers, hun. His pulse felt slower than that to me though,' I replied.

A normal adult 'textbook' systolic blood pressure would be one hundred and twenty millimetres of mercury, or 120mmHg. A systolic below 90mmHg is considered low blood pressure, particularly if symptoms are present. Systolic means the arterial pressure during contraction of the heart. It is measured in 'millimetres of mercury', pertaining to the fact that sphygmomanometers – the equipment used for measuring blood pressure – historically contained mercury, hence the letters 'mmHg' following the preceding figure.

George's sats were a little low at ninety-six percent, considering he was inhaling Entonox, which contains oxygen. However, I wasn't overly concerned by that measurement. My main concern was George's blood pressure, as it was quite low for his age. Normally, paramedics would administer a dose of GTN to a patient with chest pain of cardiac origin, because, as already mentioned, GTN is a vasodilator which dilates the arteries; that alone can reduce chest pain as more oxygenated blood can reach the tissues of the heart, feeding it with the nutrients it needs to sustain its pumping action. But to safely administer GTN, your patient's systolic blood pressure must be above ninety, because the dilating effects of GTN can cause blood pressure to reduce significantly. George's systolic blood pressure was 100mmHg, but while that was OK, I was concerned about the correlation of his low blood pressure and slow heart rate. Administering GTN to a patient with a slow heart rate and low blood pressure could cause him to 'crash', for want of a better word. I had to consider my next step promptly but carefully.

Adele, having heard George's wife say that her husband was diabetic, gained consent and pin-pricked his finger for a drop of blood to measure his blood glucose. She then informed me that the glucometer displayed a figure of 22 millimoles per litre of blood, which is usually written as mmol/l. That was high and spoke volumes to my provisional diagnosis. You see, the cause of high blood sugar levels in a diabetic can be due to a heart attack, often a 'silent' heart attack. By silent I mean the patient does not feel chest pain. It is common for diabetics to suffer a heart attack either with or without chest pain – without chest pain due to neuropathy. Neuropathy causes impairment or even absence of various sensations, one of them being pain, so the nerves do not transmit pain sensation to the brain to be interpreted. In other cases, diabetics feel chest pain but with the absence of one or more of the other textbook signs and symptoms of a heart attack. For example: pale, sweaty and clammy skin; nausea, vomiting, double incontinence; and fear of impending doom. George did present with fear of impending doom, and was pale, sweaty and had clammy skin, but he didn't complain of nausea. And fortunately for him, Adele and me, he hadn't vomited or been incontinent of urine or faeces.

We had been on scene with George for just several minutes. Adele had already pre-empted the removal of George by carry-chair and had therefore prepared it. George may have been completely independent and able to mobilise, but allowing him to walk to the ambulance could have caused him to exert himself, which would have placed more strain on his already struggling heart, so the use of the carry-chair was an absolute necessity. George came to his feet and then sat himself on the carry-chair, still holding his fist across his chest. I wrapped him in a blanket, placed the safety strap across him and fastened it, but left his right hand free so he could continue inhaling the Entonox as he felt the need. Carefully but quickly, I wheeled him from the lounge, down the hallway, towards the front door. Adele and I then lifted the carry-chair, with George in situ, up and over the threshold and down the snow covered concrete steps. The snow was still falling heavily, so with my head down and eyes squinting I pulled the chair backwards, as opposed to the usual method of pushing the chair forward, along the driveway towards the ambulance. His concerned wife locked the front door and followed closely behind, kindly carrying some of our equipment.

For the short scurry to the ambulance, I kept a close watch on George's conscious level as best as I could, as it was dark and the street lighting was quite poor. When we reached the ambulance, Adele opened the rear saloon doors and lowered the ramp. I then pulled the chair in a reverse manner into the artificially lit saloon of the ambulance.

'OK George, can you pop yourself onto the stretcher, please,' I said, unclipping the safety straps from around him. George came to his feet and lay semi-recumbent on the stretcher, while Adele raised the ramp and shut the rear doors. George's wife, looking very troubled, sat down and kept very quiet so Adele and I could continue with our assessment and treatment. Time was of the essence and George needed to be conveyed to hospital with as little delay as possible. But before we could begin mobilising to hospital, we needed to undertake further observations on him, as one particular test required the vehicle to be stationary for it to measure accurately, and also for it to print legibly. That was a 12-Lead ECG.

A 12-Lead ECG only has 10 leads but it analyses the rhythm of the heart from 12 different angles. It is used to assist a paramedic, and various other health care professionals, to diagnose a number of cardiac conditions. However, its primary purpose is to diagnose a heart attack. So, undertaking an ECG would, in *most* cases, enable me to confirm whether George was having a heart attack or not. It would also enable me to analyse his exact heart rate, which I was certain was very slow. In addition to a 12-Lead ECG, we also had to administer further drugs, including another analgesic, as Entonox was not providing adequate pain relief for him.

With Adele by my side, I asked her to obtain IV access, which involves inserting a needle into a vein, then withdrawing the needle, leaving a clear plastic tube in place through which drugs and/or fluids can be administered. Meanwhile, I wrapped the automatic blood pressure cuff, which comes attached to the ECG monitor, around George's right arm, switched the machine on and pressed the start button. While the blood pressure cuff inflated and tightened around George's arm, I wired him up to the 12-Lead ECG monitor. Moments later, a blood pressure reading appeared on the monitor; by now his systolic measured just 80mmHg.

With that measurement noted, I then observed his heart rate on the screen. To no surprise, my suspicions were confirmed; George's heart rate was just 33 beats per minute (BPM). The monitor was only capable of showing one lead at a time, lead two by default. Nevertheless, upon pressing the 'analyse twelve lead ECG' button it would, in effect, take a 'picture' of the heart from twelve different angles, and I would be able to scrutinise each of twelve different views of the heart individually.

Adele had put a cannula into George's arm, so a patent drug route was available. If my provisional diagnosis turned out to be a definitive diagnosis, he was going to need it. With his consent, I would be administering that many drugs to him in order to save his life that, were they in tablet form, he would rattle like a tube of Smarties when he moved!

'George, I need you to keep still for me now while the ECG analyses your heart, OK? Adele, can you prepare the atropine, metoclopramide and morphine for me as quickly as you can,' I asked by way of an instruction. George took several inhalations of Entonox and then kept still. I pressed the 'analyse twelve lead' button on the monitor and waited for it to print out. Seconds later, the paper began to appear with the results. I tore the long paper strip from the monitor and opened it out in its entirety. What was displayed was no surprise to me whatsoever. I handed the strip to Adele. She glanced down at it and then looked back up at me,

'You'd better get the checklist out, mate,' Adele said, as she stood preparing the drugs I'd requested.

Before I informed George that I had good reason to suspect that he was having a heart attack, and with his wife sat down behind me oblivious to my intentions, I went through a twenty-point checklist of questions to ensure that George met the criteria for thrombolysis. Thrombolysis is a pharmacological procedure which involves administering, via an intravenous route, a drug that costs between £350 and £600 a shot. Tenecteplase – more commonly known to health care professionals as TNK – is a clot-busting drug. If successful, it literally dissolves the clot in the recipient's coronary artery.

Today, most patients will not receive pre-hospital thrombolysis but instead be conveyed by ambulance, under emergency driving conditions, to a catheter laboratory. There they will have an invasive procedure called Primary Percutaneous Coronary Intervention (PPCI). That involves reopening the blocked coronary artery with a 'balloon' and placing one or more stents in the culprit artery. This restores blood supply to the part of the heart that is starved of oxygenated blood. I've watched the procedure being carried out, it's intriguing and the surgeons are without a doubt very clever people indeed.

Following nineteen of twenty positive ticks on the checklist, it was *almost* confirmed that George met the criteria to receive TNK from me, as long as I administered a drug that has a pharmacological purpose of increasing the heart rate and blood pressure. That drug was atropine. Atropine is derived from the plant, *Deadly Nightshade*. It gets its title from the 'correct' name for Deadly Nightshade – *Atropa belladonna*. If I administered atropine to George, it would have to have the desired effect on him in order for me to administer TNK through his veins.

I broke the news to George that I strongly suspected that he was having a heart attack, and that I would like to administer a drug which can destroy the clot that was occluding an artery in his heart. I also had to inform George that a potential side effect of the drug could cause a stroke, which may or may not kill him. Conversely, I also had to explain to him that if he withheld consent for me to thrombolyse him, then the heart attack *could* kill him anyway. That explanation wasn't me being unsympathetic or blunt, it was procedure and his basic human right. A patient has the right to know what the risks are of consenting to such treatment, and the risks associated with refusing treatment too.

George consented, but first I had to administer some atropine through the cannula, so Adele passed me the pre-filled syringe of atropine. I opened up the injection port of the cannula and squeezed 500 micrograms of atropine through his veins, watching the monitor closely for an increase in heart rate, as the drug often takes effect quickly. Administering atropine to your patient is, in effect, like injecting poison into them; it feels quite eerie really, poisoning a patient in order to save their life, but that's what's fascinating about medicine. What would we do without pharmacists and researchers, hey? They're absolutely brilliant!

With my eyes fixed on the monitor, George's heart rate gradually increased to 57 BPM. 'Brilliant,' I thought. I measured George's blood pressure for a third time. That too had increased, to 110mmHg. Adele then passed me the drugs that she had prepared for me moments earlier; they were metoclopramide – an anti-sickness/nausea drug – and morphine. My intention was to reduce George's pain score to a zero, if possible, before I pushed the TNK drug through the cannula in his arm. So I initially administered 10 milligrams of metoclopramide over two minutes, followed by an initial 2.5 milligrams dose of morphine. Laying semi-recumbent on the stretcher, George informed me that he could no longer tolerate inhaling Entonox, therefore I replaced the oxygen he was getting from the Entonox with supplemental oxygen via a face mask.

Thus far, he had received Entonox, oxygen, aspirin, atropine, metoclopramide and morphine. His pain score had only reduced to a five out of ten following the initial dose of the opiate-based analgesic. I pondered for a moment, 'Should I give him some GTN? Doing so would act as another analgesic, as more oxygenated blood would reach his struggling heart, but it may also lower his blood pressure again due to its effect on the arteries. Then again, if it did, I could add a little more atropine to the cocktail of drugs I'd already administered.' So I momentarily removed the O2 mask from George's face and sprayed a dose of GTN under his tongue, followed by a further 2.5 milligrams of IV morphine. Administering that second dose required me to closely monitor his respiratory rate and sats.

Adele, knowing full well that George had met the criteria to receive the TNK, had prepared the appropriate dose for his estimated weight, and also the correct dose of the drug heparin. Heparin is a blood thinning drug, similar to warfarin, and is used alongside TNK. Prior to administering TNK, heparin is given via the IV route.

I held the heparin syringe in my right hand and glanced at George again; he was still sweaty and clammy but appeared better than he had when we first arrived at his side. His improved appearance was due to the morphine, Entonox, oxygen and an increased heart rate and blood pressure from the effects of atropine. I glanced at the ECG print-out laid flat on the work surface in the saloon of the ambulance. Despite the fact that Adele, also a paramedic, believed George was having a heart attack, for a moment I doubted both hers and my own diagnosis. I glanced at the ECG once again to reaffirm to myself that it definitely displayed the signs of a massive heart attack. 'Yes, I'm sure of it,' I thought, as last second nerves tried to get the better of me.

It's not as if it was the first time I'd diagnosed a heart attack or treated a patient with TNK, but it was nerve-wracking every time the predicament arose. The patient's life is not only in your hands but heavily reliant on your level of understanding of patient presentations, signs, symptoms, and your skill, knowledge and ability to interpret the ECG. It's also an unpleasant feeling knowing that once the drug is pushed through the patient's veins, you can't take it back out. If my diagnosis was wrong and George's ashen, sweaty and clammy appearance was due to another cause, and what appeared on his ECG print-out was actually caused by another condition commonly known as an MI imposter, then pushing the drug through could potentially cost George his life. But every second that went by meant a part of George's heart was being starved of oxygen, so I just had to trust my knowledge and skills, go with my gut instinct, and just do it. After all, there is a saying in the medical profession, '*if it looks like a duck, quacks like a duck and tastes good with orange sauce, then it's a duck*'.

With that saying flooding my mind, I flicked open the cap of the cannula and held the syringe in my right hand, then positioned it vertically into the injection port. 'Here we go,' I thought. As I squeezed the pump of the syringe, well aware that my hands were shaking and my heart rate had increased with the circumstantial adrenaline flow, I watched the contents of heparin empty into George's veins. Then, I flushed the drug through with a little sodium chloride. Adele then passed me the syringe containing the TNK. With my hands still shaking a little, I immediately squeezed the TNK through the cannula, once again followed by a small amount of flush. The contents were gone. There was no going back now, and no way to remove the clot-busting drug from George's circulatory system.

'That's it, George,' I said, alternating my gaze between him and his wife, 'the clot-busting drug is in your veins, so relax as best you can and let it do its job.'

We'd been treating George in the back of the ambulance for fifteen minutes when Adele peered outside through the saloon window.

'Bloody 'ell, we'd better get moving, Andy,' she said, with a look of concern on her face because of how much snow had fallen since we had mobilised from the ambulance station.

'OK, you jump up front then and alert the CCU for me, will you. I'll give you a shout when I'm ready to move off,' I said. By CCU I meant the Cardiac Care Unit. At the time, that was the normal place to convey a patient who had been diagnosed in a pre-hospital environment as having a heart attack, and had received TNK. Adele vacated the saloon of the ambulance and sat in the cab, waiting for the go ahead from me. I made sure George had enough blankets and was warm and comfortable, and also that he and his wife were safely strapped in.

'OK Adele, when you're ready!' I shouted. She turned the ignition, revved the engine, took the handbrake off and simultaneously tried to find the bite point between the accelerator and clutch, but there was no movement. 'When you're ready, Adele!' I repeated, thinking she hadn't heard me. There was still no movement.

'Andy!' Adele shouted. I got out of my seat and popped my head through the open, sliding glass window that separates the cab from the saloon.

'What's up?' I asked.

'The ambo's stuck, it won't move!' she informed me.

'Shit!' I thought, but quietly said, 'You are joking, aren't you? Please tell me you've just got a sick sense of humour.' That wouldn't have surprised me; paramedics tend to have just that, often worse than sick – dark and twisted in fact!

'No, I'm not joking, it won't move,' she said. My mind began to race. George needed to get to hospital as soon as possible, as the doctors would need to administer a subsequent dose of heparin to him through a drip a short time after receiving pre-hospital TNK. They also needed to obtain blood samples and undertake further ECGs to see whether the clot-busting drug had been successful or not.

'Right, jump in the back, I'll have a look outside,' I said to Adele.

She got out of the cab and entered the vehicle's saloon, while I stepped out and had a look at the position we were in. On inspection, it became apparent that we were stuck because the heavily falling snow had accumulated around the wheels of the ambulance. It was then that it dawned on me that we wouldn't be able to move without some help. I stepped back into the rear of the ambulance and said to Adele,

'We're going nowhere. I'm gonna contact Control and ask them to send another crew, or if none are available to attend immediately, then send the traffic police instead.'

If another crew was available, we would simply transfer George into their ambulance and they would convey him to hospital. Failing that, as the traffic police carry shovels for scooping up glass, car debris, eyeballs and other body parts from road traffic collisions, waiting a short time for the police was the next best option. So that's what I did, explaining the situation to ambulance control, including the fact that I'd given George TNK, amongst a concoction of other drugs too. There was no additional crew available. So, as it was a dire emergency, I asked them to send the traffic police on blue lights, preferably a motorway Range Rover in case we needed pulling out of the snow. I also asked them to contact the CCU department and explain the delay to them.

With my request carried out, all that could be done was to wait and monitor George for any improving or deteriorating signs and symptoms. While I went outside to try to clear some of the snow with my feet and hands, Adele undertook further periodic measurements of George's blood pressure, and printed several more ECGs to analyse whether any post-administration of TNK improvements were evident.

Ten minutes went by before I saw blue flashing lights approaching from the distance. It was the traffic police. They hadn't come in a Range Rover, they'd come in a Volvo Estate. Nevertheless, they carried shovels and that's all that mattered. When they rolled up on scene I liaised with them and explained the predicament we were in. They then rapidly began to clear snow from around the wheels of the ambulance with their trusty shovels. Meanwhile, I stepped back into the saloon of the ambulance to allow Adele to take her position back in the driver's seat.

While waiting for the snow to be cleared, I alternated my gaze between George, his wife and Adele sat in the cab. As the minutes passed, George began to look pale, sweaty and a little vacant. Then, to my horror, his eyes closed and he slumped to one side. The warning alarms rang out on the ECG monitor. George was in cardiac arrest!

'Oh shit!' I thought, but instead shouted, 'Adele, get in the back, quick!'

'Oh god, what's happening?! George... oh god, what's happened?!' his wife cried out. Ignoring her, I glanced at the ECG monitor and immediately recognised that George's heart had deteriorated into Ventricular Fibrillation (VF). Adrenaline hurtled through my veins as I dropped the back of the stretcher down so George was laid flat. Then, using the bottom of my closed fist in a downward motion, I rapidly applied a pre-cordial thump to George's chest. A pre-cordial thump is intended to mimic what a

189

defibrillator does to the heart, with a lot less energy and effect but it does occasionally work if applied almost immediately after a patient has arrested. On this occasion, it didn't! Adele leapt into the ambulance from the side door while I was applying the defibrillator pads to George's chest.

'What's happened?' she asked.

'He's in VF, I'm gonna shock him. Get the bag and mask out will you,' I said in a fast tone, pre-empting that we might need it. I turned to George's distraught wife and said, 'Stay calm for me, OK, stay calm.'

That was easy for me to say, but not so easy or pleasant for a lady to see her husband die right in front of her very own eyes and then, in simple terms, be about to see him electrocuted. As oxygen is a combustible gas, I removed the oxygen mask from his face for safety purposes, then switched the dial on the monitor to *'pads'* and immediately pressed the *'charge'* button.

'Charging!' I said out loud as a warning. Seconds later, the audible warning sounds echoed around the ambulance, informing me as the user that the appropriate energy had charged. 'Charged, stand clear, I'm clear!' I pressed the *'shock'* button. An electrical current passed through George's body, causing his torso to lift an inch or so off the stretcher, which was normal during defibrillation. However, to George's wife it was so traumatising that she let out an almighty scream that, with our backs to her, made me and Adele jump with fright. 'Jesus!' I thought, 'Don't do that! My heart is already trying to escape from inside my chest without any more of a fright, thank you very much.'

Immediately after applying the shock, Adele and I checked the monitor, and to our joy the rhythm was back to a perfusing rhythm compatible with life. Before I even had chance to check George's carotid pulse in his neck, his eyes opened. He was oblivious to what had just happened, and was curious as to why his wife was so upset. By now sweating a little, I let out a big sigh of relief and then raised the back of the stretcher, restoring it to a semi-recumbent position. Adele, also sweating and shaking, comforted

George's distraught wife.

Due to George's brief encounter with the afterlife, I printed another ECG and measured his blood pressure, while explaining to him what had just happened. To no surprise, he was shocked (pardon the pun) by my explanation of events.

What had happened to George can occur following the administering of TNK, although it hadn't happened before to other patients I'd thrombolysed, so it had taken me a little by surprise. However, it had been emphasised during thrombolysis training that whenever the drug actually achieves its purpose – i.e. successfully destroys a clot in the coronary artery – it causes an increase in oxygen delivery (reperfusion) to the heart muscle which can sometimes cause the heart to go in to an arrhythmia – in George's case, VF. The reason a single 'shock' restored his heart to a rhythm compatible with life, and also him becoming immediately conscious, was because defibrillation was carried out within seconds of him arresting. It is seldom successful if there is any considerable delay in defibrillating a patient who has been in a VF cardiac arrest for more than a few minutes, which is why pre-hospital cardiac arrest statistics are, unfortunately, very poor.

I learnt from that experience, and so I now place the defibrillation pads on all patients who are having a heart attack – in fact any patient who is at risk of deteriorating in to cardiac arrest – thus preventing any delay in 'shocking' the patient due to time spent applying the pads.

With normality restored, George's wife asked if her husband was going to be alright. I had to be honest with her and so tactfully explained that we needed to get him to hospital as fast as possible in order to increase his chance of survival in the long-term. Adele liaised with the police officers for a brief moment and then took her position back in the driver's seat and I gave her the all clear to move off. She revved the engine, took the handbrake off and found the bite between the accelerator and the clutch, and fortunately the vehicle moved away from the side of the road. Adele waved at the cavalry as she drove off,

'Thank you!' she shouted out of the window. The police were completely unaware of what had happened moments before.

Progressing slowly along the road towards the hospital, I closely monitored George's vital signs, including his ECG rhythm, and periodically comforted George's distraught wife at the same time. What appeared on the ECG was encouraging; the signs of a heart attack were gradually reducing. Thankfully, the drug was serving its purpose. George's pain score had by now reduced to a zero due to the analgesia administered and the clot-busting drug having a positive effect on the flow of oxygen to his heart. His colour had also improved and he had become a lot less sweaty and clammy, and George's facial expression appeared to show that of a man who wasn't so frightened anymore. The treatment administered was having a positive effect all round.

When we arrived at the CCU department, Adele promptly vacated the cab, opened the rear doors and lowered the ramp. We quickly wheeled the stretcher into the ward, followed by George's upset wife. She was escorted by a nurse to the waiting area where a patient's loved ones are expected to wait for good or bad news from the doctors. Meanwhile, I gave a handover to the awaiting consultant.

As paramedics are usually the first health care professionals on scene and hold vital information about an incident, a doctor usually listens to a handover from the paramedic while other doctors commence the assessment and treatment of the sick or injured patient. A handover is intended to summarise the history of events and observations undertaken by the paramedic, and the treatment provided. It is not usually conveyed grammatically or in full sentences, because doing so prolongs the process; if you have requested the resuscitation room, or in this case the CCU department, to be on standby, then the doctor needs information fast! Therefore, a handover is usually passed without interruption from anyone else in the room. For the benefit of the layperson, I have simplified handovers, where appropriate, throughout this book.

As we transferred George over to the hospital bed, I began my ungrammatical handover to the attentive doctor, which went something like this:

'This is George; he's fifty-seven years old and an insulin dependent diabetic. George was woken by central chest pain radiating down his left arm and into his jaw, at about two a.m. On arrival, he was fully conscious, breathing shallow and was anxious. He was ashen in colour, sweating profusely, clammy to the touch and complained of a pain score of ten, which he had experienced for approximately one hour by the time we had arrived at his side.

'Entonox initially administered, to some relief, and an aspirin was given too. George had a weak, slow pulse and an initial systolic blood pressure of one hundred, so GTN withheld, due to an unconfirmed heart attack in the lower portion of the heart.

'On further examination, his heart rate was thirty-three beats per minute. BP reduced to eighty systolic. His blood glucose was twenty-two, and his twelve lead ECG displayed signs of a heart attack.

'IV access obtained and five hundred micrograms of atropine administered to good effect. Heart rate increased to fifty-seven and systolic blood pressure increased to one hundred and ten, so a dose of GTN administered.

'George met all of the criteria for thrombolysis, so post atropine he received metoclopramide, morphine, heparin and TNK, but during the delay on scene deteriorated in to a VF arrest. A pre-cordial thump was applied and a single shock was delivered. George immediately regained consciousness and was oblivious to the event.

'Further ECGs undertaken, and the most current is showing an improvement in heart tissue perfusion. Current pain score zero out of ten. Are there any questions?'

'No, thank you,' the doctor replied.

The CCU staff then continued with George's assessment,

undertaking further post-thrombolysis observations on him. Adele and I went back out to the ambulance for some much needed fresh air. It was a relief to have got George into hospital alive, although he wasn't completely out of the woods yet, as the saying goes. He had a high chance of going in to cardiac arrest again at any time, until the occlusion in his coronary artery had completely dispersed or, as mentioned earlier, PPCI had been performed by surgeons.

After completing my documentation detailing the events that had occurred, Adele and I informed ambulance control that we were clear from hospital, and so we returned to station for a brew.

The following night, while at the same hospital and once again working with Adele, we decided to visit George in the CCU department before it got too late. Before visiting him at his bedside, I asked a duty nurse how George was. She informed me that thrombolysis had been successful and that he'd received PPCI too and was on the road to recovery, which was music to my ears given the predicament we had been in the previous night. After speaking with the nurse, Adele and I approached George, who was sat up in bed relaxing. He looked a picture of health compared to the previous night. He clearly remembered both of us and offered us his hand, and at the same time said,

'Thank you both for saving my life last night.'

'You're welcome,' I replied. 'But can I ask you a question out of intrigue; well, more so morbid curiosity really?'

'Of course,' he said.

'You know you hear stories about people in cardiac arrest looking down on themselves, say for instance, from the corner of a room, being resuscitated by medics and lay people, etcetera?'

'Yeah,' he replied, nodding his head.

'Well, did you see "the light"?' I asked, using flexed index and middle fingers of my hands to emphasise quotation marks. 'Or did you experience seeing any deceased relatives that told you to go back because it's not your time yet, or anything else?'

194

'No, nothing, just blackout, that's it,' he replied.

Available in Paperback, Digital and Audio Download

The Dark Side

Part 2

Real Life Accounts of an NHS Paramedic

The Traumatic, the Tragic and the Tearful

www.andythompson-author.com

Lightning Source UK Ltd.
Milton Keynes UK
UKOW06f0603010917
308393UK00011B/383/P